D1291320

INTERPRETATION THEORY

INTERPRETATION THEORY:
Discourse and the Surplus of Meaning

Paul Ricoeur

Fort Worth, Texas

Copyright © 1976 TCU Press
All rights reserved

The Library of Congress Cataloged the First Issue of this work as
follows:
  Ricoeur, Paul.
    Interpretation theory: discourse and the surplus of meaning
    Paul Ricoeur. —Fort Worth: Texas Christian University
    Press, c1976.
    xii, 107 p.: port.: 24 cm
    1. Discourse analysis—Addresses, essays, lectures.
    2. Meaning (Philosophy) Addresses, essays, lectures.
    3. Languages—Philosophy—Addresses, essays, lectures.
    I. Title
    P302.R5   410   76-29604
    ISBN 0-912646-25X   MARC
    ISBN 0-912646-59-4
    ISBN 978-0-912646-59-6

TCU Press
P.O. Box 298300
Fort Worth, Texas 76129
817.257.7822
www.prs.tcu.edu
To order books: 1.800.826.8911

Paul Ricoeur

PREFACE

IN THE FALL OF 1973 Paul Ricoeur journeyed from Paris to Fort Worth to deliver a series of lectures as part of the centennial celebration of Texas Christian University. That series bore the title "Discourse and the Surplus of Meaning." The expanded text published here under the title *Interpretation Theory* retains the earlier title as a subtitle. This change marks the development of the text into a systematic and comprehensive theory that attempts to account for the unity of human language in view of the diverse uses to which it is put.

A reasonable question is that of the location of this text within the horizon of Ricoeur's investigations of language and discourse published after *The Symbolism of Evil* (1960). That broad horizon is the search for a comprehensive philosophy of language that can account for the multiple functions of the human act of signifying and for all their interrelations. No single work published during this period (1960-1969) claims to offer that comprehensive philosophy, and no claim is made that the investigations, taken together, constitute it, for Ricoeur doubts that it could be elaborated by a single thinker.

How does *Interpretation Theory* stand in regard to this search? It occupies a distinct place, for works such as *Freud and Philosophy* (1965) and *The Conflict of Interpretations* (1969) are mainly investigations of the diverse uses to which language as discourse is put, while *Interpretation Theory* offers an account of the unity of human language in view of this diversity of function. In his *Interpretation Theory* we have Paul Ricoeur's philosophy of integral language.

As a result of the initial lecture presentation, a workshop on the interpretation of texts and a symposium on language were held at Texas Christian University in 1975. Professor Ricoeur returned to TCU for these events and developed his theory by offering critiques of the papers presented by TCU faculty and graduate students from widely diverse disciplines. These events indicate the power of this theory of interpretation and philosophy of language. It is our intention to make it available now to a much wider audience through this publication of the expanded version of Paul Ricoeur's Centennial Lectures at TCU.

This University sought the best in contemporary scholarship to help celebrate its centennial and thus properly honored Professor Ricoeur by the invitation. In turn, he offered his best scholarship and thus honored the University and helped to celebrate its centennial fittingly. We are grateful.

Ted Klein
Chairman, Department of Philosophy
Texas Christian University
Fort Worth, Texas

CONTENTS

INTRODUCTION

THE FOUR ESSAYS that make up this volume are based upon and expand the lectures I delivered at Texas Christian University, 27-30 November 1973, as their Centennial Lectures. They may be read as separate essays, but they may also be read as step by step approximations of a solution to a single problem, that of understanding language at the level of such productions as poems, narratives, and essays, whether literary or philosophical. In other words, the central problem at stake in these four essays is that of works; in particular, that of language as *a work*.

A complete grasp of this problem is not achieved until the fourth essay, which deals with the two apparently conflicting attitudes that we may assume when dealing with language as a work; I mean the apparent conflict between explanation and understanding. I believe, however, that this conflict is only an apparent one and that it may be overcome if these two attitudes can be shown to be dialectically related to each other. Hence it is this dialectic which constituted the horizon of my lectures.

If the dialectic between explanation and understanding may be said to provide the ultimate reference of my remarks, the first step taken in its direction must be a decisive one: we must cross the threshold beyond which language stands as *discourse*. Accordingly, the topic of the first essay is that of language as discourse. But, to the extent that only written language fully displays the criteria of discourse, a second investigation concerns the amplitude of the changes that affect discourse when it is no longer spoken, but written. Hence the title of my second essay, "Speaking and Writing."

The theory of the text, which emerges from this discussion, is advanced a step further with the question of the *plurivocity* belonging not only to words (polysemy), or even to sentences (ambiguity), but to full works of discourse such as poems, narratives, and essays. This problem of plurivocity, discussed in the third essay, provides the decisive transition to the problem of interpretation ruled by the dialectic of explanation and understanding, which I have indicated is the horizon of this whole set of essays.

I wish to express my gratitude and thanks to the people of Texas Christian University for the opportunity they extended me of delivering the lectures that form the basis of this work and also for their gracious hospitality during my stay there. I was pleased to be able to contribute to their centennial celebration.

1.

LANGUAGE AS DISCOURSE

THE TERMS IN WHICH THE PROBLEM of language as discourse will be discussed in this essay are modern in the sense that they could not have been adequately formulated without the tremendous progress of modern linguistics. Yet if the terms are modern, the problem itself is not a new one. It has always been known. In the *Cratylus*, Plato had already shown that the problem of the "truth" of isolated words or names must remain undecided because naming does not exhaust the power or the function of speaking. The *logos* of language requires at least a name and a verb, and it is the intertwining of these two words which constitutes the first unit of language and thought. Even this unit only raises a claim to truth; the question must still be decided in each instance.

The same problem recurs in the more mature works of Plato such as the *Theaetetus* and the *Sophist*. There the question is to understand how error is possible, i.e., how it is possible to say what is not the case, if to speak always means to say something. Plato is again compelled to conclude that a word by itself is neither true nor false, although a combination of words may mean something yet grasp nothing. The bearer of this paradox, once again, is the sentence, not the word.

Such is the first context within which the concept of discourse was discovered: error and truth are "affections" of discourse, and discourse requires two basic signs — a noun and a verb — which are connected in a synthesis which goes beyond the words. Aristotle says the same thing in his treatise *On Interpretation*. A noun has a meaning and a verb has, in

1

addition to its meaning, an indication of time. Only their conjunction brings forth a predicative link, which can be called *logos*, discourse. It is this synthetic unit which carries the double act of assertion and denial. An assertion may be contradicted by another assertion, and it may be true or false.

This short summary of the archaic stage of our problem is intended to remind us of both the antiquity and the continuity of the problem of language as discourse. However, the terms within which we shall now discuss it are quite new because they take into account the methodology and discoveries of modern linguistics.

In terms of this linguistics, the problem of discourse has become a genuine problem because discourse now can be opposed to a contrary term, which was not recognized or was taken for granted by the ancient philosophers. This opposite term today is the autonomous object of scientific investigation. It is the linguistic code which gives a specific structure to each of the linguistic systems, which we know as the various languages spoken by different linguistic communities. Language here then means something other than the general capacity to speak or the common competence of speaking. It designates the particular structure of the particular linguistic system.

With the words "structure" and "system" a new problematic emerges which tends, at least initially, to postpone, if not cancel, the problem of discourse, which is condemned to recede from the forefront of concern and become a residual problem. If discourse remains problematic for us today, it is because the main achievements of linguistics concern language as structure and system and not as used. Our task therefore will be to rescue discourse from its marginal and precarious exile.

Langue and *Parole:* The Structural Model

The withdrawal of the problem of discourse in the contemporary study of language is the price we must pay for the tremendous achievements brought about by the famous *Cours de linguistique général* of the Swiss linguist Ferdinand de Saussure.[1] His work relies on a fundamental distinction between language as *langue* and as *parole*, which has strongly shaped modern linguistics. (Note that Saussure did not speak of "discourse," but of "*parole*." Later we shall understand why.) *Langue* is the code—or the set of codes—on the basis of which a particular speaker produces *parole* as a particular message.

To this main dichotomy are connected several subsidiary distinctions. A message is individual, its code is collective. (Strongly influenced by Durkheim, Saussure considered linguistics to be a branch of sociology.) The message and the code do not belong to time in the same way. A message is a temporal event in the succession of events which constitute the diachronic dimension of time, while the code is in time as a set of contemporaneous elements, i.e., as a synchronic system. A message is intentional; it is meant by someone. The code is anonymous and not intended. In this sense it is unconscious, not in the sense that drives and impulses are unconscious according to Freudian metapsychology, but in the sense of a nonlibidinal structural and cultural unconscious.

More than anything else, a message is arbitrary and contingent, while a code is systematic and compulsory for a given speaking community. This last opposition is reflected in the affinity of a code for scientific investigation; particularly in a sense of the word science which emphasizes the quasialgebraic level of the combinatory capacities implied by such finite sets of discrete entities as phonological, lexical, and syntactical systems. Even if *parole* can be scientifically described, it falls under many sciences including acoustics, physiology, sociology, and the history of semantic changes, whereas *langue* is the object of a single science, the description of the *synchronic systems* of language.

This rapid survey of the main dichotomies established by Saussure is sufficient to show why linguistics could make progress under the condition of bracketing the message for the sake of the code, the event for the sake of the system, the intention for the sake of the structure, and the arbitrariness of the act for the systematicity of combinations within synchronic systems.

3

The eclipse of discourse was further encouraged by the tentative extension of the structural model beyond its birth place in linguistics properly speaking, and by the systematic awareness of the theoretical requirements implied by the linguistic model as a structural model.

Extension of the structural model concerns us directly insofar as the structural model was applied to the same categories of texts that are the object of our interpretation theory. Originally the model concerned units smaller than the sentence, the signs of the lexical systems and the discrete units of the phonological systems from which the significant units of lexical systems are compounded. A decisive extension occurred, however, with the application of the structural model to linguistic entities larger than the sentence and also to non-linguistic entities similar to the texts of linguistic communication.

As concerns the first type of application, the treatment of folktales by the Russian formalists such as V. Propp[2] marks a decisive turn in the theory of literature, especially as regards the narrative structure of literary works. The application of the structural model to myths by Claude Lévi-Strauss constitutes a second example of a structural approach to long strings of discourse; an approach similar to, yet independent of the formal treatment of folklore proposed by the Russian formalists.

As concerns the extension of the structural model to non-linguistic entities, the application may be less spectacular — including as it does, road signals, cultural codes such as table manners, costume, building and dwelling codes, decorative patterns, etc.—but it is theoretically interesting in that it gives an empirical content to the concept of semiology or general semantics, which was developed independently by Saussure and Charles S. Pierce. Linguistics here becomes one province of the general theory of signs, albeit a province that has the privilege of being both one species and the paradigmatic example of a sign-system.

This last extension of the structural model already implies a theoretical apprehension of the postulates that govern semiology in general and structural linguistics in particular.

4

Taken together, these postulates define and describe the structural model as a model.

First, a synchronic approach must precede any diachronic approach because systems are more intelligible than changes. At best, a change is a partial or a global change in a state of a system. Therefore the history of changes must come after the theory that describes the synchronic states of the system. This first postulate expresses the emergence of a new type of intelligibility directly opposed to the historicism of the nineteenth century.

Second, the paradigmatic case for a structural approach is that of a finite set of discrete entities. At first glance, phonological systems may seem to satisfy this second postulate more directly than do lexical systems where the criterion of finiteness is more difficult to apply concretely. However, the idea of an infinite lexicon remains absurd in principle. This theoretical advantage of phonological systems — only a few dozen distinctive signs characterize any given linguistic system — explains why phonology moved to the forefront of linguistic studies following Saussure's work, even though for the founder of structural linguistics, phonology was taken to be an auxiliary science to the core of linguistics: semantics. The paradigmatic position of systems constituted of finite sets of discrete entities lies in the combinatory capacity and the quasi-algebraic possibilities pertaining to such sets. These capacities and possibilities add to the type of intelligibility instituted by the first postulate, that of synchronicity.

Third, in such a system no entity belonging to the structure of the system has a meaning of its own; the meaning of a word, for example, results from its opposition to the other lexical units of the same system. As Saussure said, in a system of signs there are only differences, but no substantial existence. This postulate defines the formal properties of linguistic entities, formal here being opposed to substantial in the sense of an autonomous positive existence of the entities at stake in linguistics and, in general, in semiotics.

Fourth, in such finite systems, all the relations are immanent to the system. In this sense semiotic systems are "closed," i.e., without relations to external, non-semiotic real-

5

ity. The definition of the sign given by Saussure already implied this postulate: instead of being defined by the external relation between a sign and a thing, a relation that would make linguistics dependent upon a theory of extra-linguistic entities, the sign is defined by an opposition between two aspects, which both fall within the circumspection of a unique science, that of signs. These two aspects are the signifier—for example, a sound, a written pattern, a gesture, or any physical medium — and the signified — the differential value in the lexical system. The fact that the signifier and the signified allow for two different kinds of analysis—phonological in the first case, semantical in the second—but only together constitute the sign, not only provides the criterion for linguistic signs, but also, by extension, that of the entities of every semiotic system, which may be defined on the condition of "weakening" this criterion.

The last postulate alone suffices to characterize structuralism as a global mode of thought, beyond all the technicalities of its methodology. Language no longer appears as a mediation between minds and things. It constitutes a world of its own, within which each item only refers to other items of the same system, thanks to the interplay of oppositions and differences constitutive of the system. In a word, language is no longer treated as a "form of life," as Wittgenstein would call it, but as a self-sufficient system of inner relationships.

At this extreme point language as discourse has disappeared.

Semantics versus Semiotics: The Sentence

To this unidimensional approach to language, for which signs are the only basic entities, I want to oppose a two dimensional approach for which language relies on two irreducible entities, signs and sentences.

This duality does not coincide with that of *langue* and *parole* as defined in Saussure's *Cours de linguistique générale*, or even as that duality was later reformulated as the opposition between code and message. In the terminology of *langue* and *parole*, only *langue* is an homogeneous object for a unique science, thanks to the structural properties of the synchronic systems. *Parole*, as we said, is heterogeneous, besides being individual, diachronic, and contingent. But *parole* also presents a structure that is irreducible in a specific sense to that of the combinatory possibilities opened up by the oppositions between discrete entities. This structure is the synthetic construction of the sentence itself as distinct from any analytic combination of discrete entities. My substitution of the term "discourse" for that of *"parole"* (which expresses only the residual aspect of a science of *"langue"*) is intended not only to emphasize the specificity of this new unit on which all discourse relies, but also to legitimate the distinction between semiotics and semantics as the two sciences which correspond to the two kinds of units characteristic of language, the sign and the sentence.

Moreover, these two sciences are not just distinct, but also reflect a hierarchical order. The object of semiotics — the sign — is merely virtual. Only the sentence is actual as the very event of speaking. This is why there is no way of passing from the word as a lexical sign to the sentence by mere extension of the same methodology to a more complex entity. The sentence is not a larger or more complex word, it is a new entity. It may be decomposed into words, but the words are something other than short sentences. A sentence is a whole irreducible to the sum of its parts. It is made up of words, but it is not a derivative function of its words. A sentence is made up of signs, but is not itself a sign.

There is therefore no linear progression from the phoneme to the lexeme and then on to the sentence and to linguistic wholes larger than the sentence. Each stage requires new structures and a new description. The relation between the two kinds of entities may be expressed in the following way, following the French Sanskritist Emile Benveniste: language relies on the possibility of two kinds of operations, integration into larger wholes, and dissociation into constitutive parts. The sense proceeds from the first operation, the form from the second.

7

The distinction between two kinds of linguistics — semiotics and semantics — reflects this network of relations. Semiotics, the science of signs, is formal to the extent that it relies on the dissociation of language into constitutive parts. Semantics, the science of the sentence, is immediately concerned with the concept of sense (which at this stage can be taken as synonymous with meaning, before the forthcoming distinction between sense and reference is introduced), to the extent that semantics is fundamentally defined by the integrative procedures of language.

For me, the distinction between semantics and semiotics is the key to the whole problem of language, and my four essays are based upon this initial methodological decision. As I said in my introductory remarks, this distinction is simply a reassessment of the argument of Plato in the *Cratylus* and the *Theaetetus* according to which the *logos* relies on the intertwining of at least two different entities, the noun and the verb. But, in another sense, this distinction today requires more sophistication because of the existence of semiotics as the modern counterpart of semantics.

The Dialectic of Event and Meaning

The next part of this essay will be devoted to the search for adequate criteria to differentiate semantics and semiotics. I shall construct my arguments from the convergence of several approaches, which have to do for different reasons with the specificity of language as discourse. Those approaches are the linguistics of the sentence that provide the general title semantics; the phenomenology of meaning proceeding from the first *Logical Investigation* of Husserl;[3] and the kind of "linguistic analysis" that characterizes the Anglo-American philosophical description of "ordinary language." All these partial achievements will be gathered under a common title, the dialectic of event and meaning in discourse, for which I shall first describe the event pole, then the meaning pole as the abstract components of this concrete polarity.

Discourse as Event

Starting from the Saussurean distinction between *langue* and *parole*, we may say, at least in an introductory way, that discourse is *the* event of language. For a linguistics applied to the structure of systems, the temporal dimension of this event expresses the epistemological weakness of a linguistics of *parole*. Events vanish while systems remain. Therefore the first move of a semantics of discourse must be to rectify this epistemological weakness of *parole* proceeding from the fleeting character of the event as opposed to the stability of the system by relating it to the ontological priority of discourse resulting from the actuality of the event as opposed to the mere virtuality of the system.

If it is true that only the message has a temporal existence, an existence in duration and succession, the synchronistic aspect of the code putting the system outside of successive time, then this temporal existence of the message testifies to its actuality. The system in fact does not exist. It only has a virtual existence. Only the message gives actuality to language, and discourse grounds the very existence of language since only the discrete and each time unique acts of discourse actualize the code.

But this first criterion alone would be more misleading than illuminating if the "instance of discourse," as Benveniste calls it, were merely this vanishing event. Then science would be justified in discarding it, and the ontological priority of discourse would be insignificant and without consequence. An act of discourse is not merely transitory and vanishing, however. It may be identified and reidentified as the same so that we may say it again or in other words. We may even say it in another language or translate it from one language into another. Through all these transformations it preserves an identity of its own which can be called the propositional content, the "said as such."

We therefore have to reformulate our first criterion — discourse as event—in a more dialectical way in order to take into account the relation which constitutes discourse as such, the relation between event and meaning. But before being able to grasp this dialectic as a whole, let us consider the "objective" side of the speech event.

Discourse as Predication

Considered from the point of view of the propositional content, the sentence may be characterized by a single distinctive trait: it has a predicate. As Benveniste observes, even the grammatical subject may be lacking, but not the predicate. What is more, this new unit is not defined by its opposition to other units, as a phoneme to another phoneme or a lexeme to another lexeme within the same system. There are not several kinds of predicates; at the level of categoremes (*categorema*, in Greek = *praedicatum*, in Latin), there is just one kind of linguistic utterance, the proposition, which constitutes just one class of distinctive units. Consequently, there is no unit of a higher order that could provide a generic class for the sentence conceived as a species. It is possible to connect propositions according to an order of concatenation, but not to integrate them.

This linguistic criterion may be related to descriptions established by the theorists of ordinary language. The predicate, which Benveniste says is the only indispensable factor of the sentence, makes sense in those paradigmatic cases where its "functions" may be connected to and opposed to the "function" of the logical subject. Then an important feature of the predicate comes to the forefront on the basis of the antithesis between predicate and subject. Whereas the genuinely logical subject is the bearer of a singular identification, what the predicate says about the subject can always be treated as a "universal" feature of the subject. Subject and predicate do not do the same job in the proposition. The subject picks out something singular — Peter, London, this table, the fall of Rome, the first man who climbed Mt. Everest, etc.—by means of several grammatical devices which serve this logical function: proper names, pronouns, demonstratives (this and that, now and then, here and there, tenses of the verb as related to the present), and "definite descriptions" (the so and so). What they all have in common is that they all identify one and only

10

one item. The predicate, in contrast, designates a kind of quality, a class of things, a type of relation, or a type of action.

This fundamental polarity between singular identification and universal predication gives a specific content to the notion of the proposition conceived of as the object of the speech event. It shows that discourse is not merely a vanishing event, and as such an irrational entity, as the simple opposition between *parole* and *langue* might suggest. Discourse has a structure of its own but it is not a structure in the analytical sense of structuralism, i.e., as a combinatory power based on the previous oppositions of discrete units. Rather, it is a structure in the synthetic sense, i.e., as the intertwining and interplay of the functions of identification and predication in one and the same sentence.

The Dialectic of Event and Meaning

Discourse considered as either an event or a proposition, that is, as a predicative function combined with an identification, is an abstraction, which depends upon the concrete whole that is the dialectical unity of the event and meaning in the sentence.

This dialectical constitution of discourse might be overlooked by a psychological or an existential approach which would concentrate on the interplay of functions, the polarity of singular identification and universal predication. It is the task of a concrete theory of discourse to take this dialectic as its guideline. Any emphasis on the abstract concept of a speech event is justified only as a way of protesting against an earlier, more abstract reduction of language, the reduction to the structural aspects of language as *langue*, for the notion of speech as an event provides the key to the transition from a linguistics of the code to a linguistics of the message. It reminds us that discourse is realized temporally and in a present moment, whereas the language system is virtual and outside of time. But this trait appears only in the movement of actualization from language to discourse. Every apology for speech as an event, therefore, is significant if, and only if, it makes visible the relation of actualization, thanks to which our linguistic competence actualizes itself in performance.

11

But this same apology becomes abusive itself as soon as the event character is extended from the problematic of actualization, where it is valid, to another problematic, that of understanding. *If all discourse is actualized as an event, all discourse is understood as meaning.* By meaning or sense I here designate the propositional content, which I have just described, as the synthesis of two functions: the identification and the predication. It is not the event insofar as it is transient that we want to understand, but its meaning — the intertwining of noun and verb, to speak like Plato — insofar as it endures.

In saying this I am not taking a step backward from the linguistics of speech (or discourse) to the linguistics of language (as *langue*). It is in the linguistics of discourse that the event and the meaning are articulated. The supressing and the surpassing of the event in the meaning is a characteristic of discourse itself. It attests to the intentionality of language, the relation of noesis and noema in it. If language is a *meinen*, an intending, it is so precisely due to this *Aufhebung* through which the event is cancelled as something merely transient and retained as the *same* meaning.

Before drawing the main consequence of this dialectical interpretation of the notion of speech event for our hermeneutical enterprise, let us elaborate more completely and more concretely the dialectic itself on the basis of some important corollaries of our axiom: that if all discourse is actualized as an event, it is understood as meaning.

Utterer's Meaning and Utterance Meaning

The Self-Reference of Discourse

The concept of meaning allows two interpretations which reflect the main dialectic between event and meaning. To mean is both what the speaker means, i.e., what he intends to say, and what the sentence means, i.e., what the conjunction between the identification function and the predicative function yields. Meaning, in other words, is both noetic and noematic. We may connect the reference of discourse to its speaker with the event side of the dialectic. The event is somebody speaking. In this sense, the system or code is anonymous to the extent that it is merely virtual. Languages do not speak, people do. But the propositional side of the self-reference of discourse must not be overlooked if the utterer's meaning, to use a term of Paul Grice's, is not to be reduced to a mere psychological intention. The mental meaning can be found nowhere else than in discourse itself. The utterer's meaning has its mark in the utterance meaning. How?

The linguistics of discourse, which we are calling semantics to distinguish it from semiotics, provides the answer. The inner structure of the sentence refers back to its speaker through grammatical procedures, which linguists call "shifters." The personal pronouns, for example, have no objective meaning. "I" is not a concept. It is impossible to substitute a universal expression for it such as "the one who is now speaking." Its only function is to refer the whole sentence to the subject of the speech event. It has a new meaning each time it is used and each time it refers to a singular subject. "I" is the one who in speaking applies to himself the word "I" which appears in the sentence as a logical subject. There are other shifters, other grammatical bearers of the reference of the discourse to its speaker as well. They include the tenses of the verb to the extent that they are centered around the present and therefore refer to the "now" of the speech event and of the speaker. The same thing is true of the adverbs of time and space and the demonstratives, which may be considered as egocentric particulars. Discourse therefore has many substitutable ways of referring back to its speaker.

By paying attention to these grammatical devices of the self-reference of discourse we obtain two advantages. On the one hand, we get a new criterion of the difference between discourse and linguistic codes. On the other hand, we are able to give a nonpsychological, because purely semantic, definition of the utterer's meaning. No mental entity need be hypothesized or hypostazised. The utterance meaning points back towards the utterer's meaning thanks to the self-reference of discourse to itself as an event.

This semantic approach is reinforced by two other contributions to the same dialectic of the event and the proposition.

13

Locutionary and Illocutionary Acts.

The first one is the well known linguistic analysis (in the Anglo-American sense of this term) of the "speech-act." J. L. Austin was the first to notice that "performatives" — such as promises — imply a specific commitment by the speaker who *does* what he says in saying it. By saying, "I promise," he actually promises, i.e., puts himself under the obligation of doing what he says he will do. This "doing" of the saying may be assimilated to the event pole on the dialectic of event and meaning. But this "doing" also follows semantic rules which are exhibited by the structure of the sentence: the verb must be that of the first person indicative. Here, too, a specific "grammar" supports the performative force of the discourse. The performatives are only particular cases of a general feature exhibited by every class of speech act, whether they be commands, wishes, questions, warnings, or assertions. All of them, besides saying something (the locutionary act), do something in saying (the illocutionary act), and yield effects *by* saying (the perlocutionary act).

The illocutionary act is what distinguishes a promise from an order, a wish, or an assertion. And the "force" of the illocutionary act presents the same dialectic of event and meaning. In each case a specific "grammar" corresponds to a certain intention for which the illocutionary act expresses the distinctive "force." What can be expressed in psychological terms such as believing, wanting, or desiring, is invested with a semantic existence thanks to the correlation between these grammatical devices and the illocutionary act.

The Interlocutionary Act

The other contribution to the dialectic of the event and the propositional content is given by what could be called the interlocutionary act or the allocutionary act, to preserve the symmetry with the illocutionary aspect of the speech act.

One important aspect of discourse is that it is addressed to someone. There is another speaker who is the addressee of the discourse. The presence of the pair, speaker and hearer, constitutes language as communication. The study of language from the point of view of communication does not begin with the sociology of communication, however. As Plato says, dialogue is an essential structure of discourse. Questioning and answering sustain the movement and the dynamic of speaking, and in one sense they do not constitute one mode of discourse among others. Each illocutionary act is a kind of question. To assert something is to expect agreement, just as to give an order is to expect obedience. Even soliloquy — solitary discourse — is dialogue with oneself, or, to cite Plato once more, *dianoia* is the dialogue of the soul with itself.

Some linguists have attempted to reformulate all the functions of language as variables within an all encompassing model for which communication is the key. Roman Jakobson, for example, starts from the threefold relation between speaker, hearer, and message, then adds three other complementary factors which enrich his model. These are code, contact, and context. On the basis of this six factor system he establishes a six function schema. To the speaker corresponds the emotive function, to the hearer the conative, to the message the poetic function. The code designates the metalinguistic function, while the contact and the context are the bearers of the phatic and the referential functions.

This model is interesting in that it (1) describes discourse directly and not as a residue of language; (2) describes a structure of discourse and not only an irrational event; and (3) it subordinates the code function to the connecting operation of communication.

But in turn this model calls for a philosophical investigation, which may be provided by the dialectic of event and meaning. For the linguist, communication is a fact, even a most obvious fact. People do actually speak to one another. But for an existential investigation communication is an enigma, even a wonder. Why? Because being-together, as the existential condition for the possibility of any dialogical structure of discourse, appears as a way of trespassing or overcoming the fundamental solitude of each human being. By solitude I do not mean that fact that we often feel isolated as in a crowd, or that we live and die alone, but, in a more radical sense, that what is experienced by one person cannot be transferred whole as such and such experience to someone

15

else. My experience cannot directly become your experience. An event belonging to one stream of consciousness cannot be transferred as such into another stream of consciousness. Yet, nevertheless, something passes from me to you. Something is transferred from one sphere of life to another. This something is not the experience as experienced, but its meaning. Here is the miracle. The experience as experienced, as lived, remains private, but its sense, its meaning, becomes public. Communication in this way is the overcoming of the radical non-communicability of the lived experience as lived.

This new aspect of the dialectic of event and meaning deserves attention. The event is not only the experience as expressed and communicated, but also the intersubjective exchange itself, the happening of dialogue. The instance of discourse is the instance of dialogue. Dialogue is an event which connects two events, that of speaking and that of hearing. It is to this dialogical event that understanding as meaning is homogeneous. Hence the question: what aspects of discourse itself are meaningfully communicated in the event of dialogue?

A first answer is obvious. What can be communicated is first of all the propositional content of discourse, and we are led back to our main criterion—discourse as event plus sense. Because the sense of a sentence is, so to speak, "external" to the sentence it can be transferred; this exteriority of discourse to itself — which is synonymous with the self-transcendence of the event in its meaning—*opens* discourse to the other. The message has the ground of its communicability in the structure of its meaning. This implies that we communicate the synthesis of both the identification function (of which the logical subject is the bearer) and the predicative function (which is potentially universal). By speaking to somebody we point towards the unique thing that we mean, thanks to the public devices of proper names, demonstratives, and definite descriptions. I help the other to identify the same item that I myself am pointing to, thanks to the grammatical devices which provide a singular experience with a public dimension.

The same is true for the universal dimension of the predicate communicated by the generic dimension of the lexical entities.

Of course, this first level of mutual understanding does not go without some misunderstanding. Most of our words are polysemic; they have more than one meaning. But it is the contextual function of discourse to screen, so to speak, the polysemy of our words and to reduce the plurality of possible interpretations, the ambiguity of discourse resulting from the unscreened polysemy of the words. And it is the function of dialogue to initiate this screening function of the context. The contextual is the dialogical. It is in this precise sense that the contextual role of dialogue reduces the field of misunderstanding concerning the propositional content and partially succeeds in overcoming the non-communicability of experience.

The propositional content is only the correlate of the locutionary act, however. What about the communicability of the other aspects of the speech act, especially the illocutionary act? It is here that the dialectic of the act and the structure, the event and the meaning, is the most complex. How can the character of discourse, which is to be either constative or performative, either an act of stating something or of ordering, wishing, promising, or warning, be communicated and understood? More radically, can we communicate the speech act as an illocutionary act?

There is no doubt that it is easier to mistake one illocutionary act for another illocutionary act than it is to misunderstand a propositional act. The main reason is that nonlinguistic facts are intertwined with the linguistic marks, and these factors—which include physiognomy, gesture, and intonation of the voice — are more difficult to interpret because they do not rely on discrete units, their codes being more unstable and their message easier to conceal or fake. Nevertheless the illocutionary act is not without linguistic marks. They include the use of grammatical moods such as the indicative, subjunctive, imperative, and optative, as well as the tenses and codified adverbial terms or other equivalent

17

periphrastic devices. Writing not only preserves these linguistic marks of oral speech, it also adds supplementary distinctive signs such as quotation marks, exclamation marks, and question marks to indicate the physiognomic and gestural expressions, which disappear when the speaker becomes a writer. In many ways therefore illocutionary acts can be communicated to the extent that their "grammar" provides the event with a public structure.

I am inclined to say that the perlocutionary act—what we do by speaking — frighten, seduce, convince, etc. — is the least communicable aspect of the speech act, inasmuch as the nonlinguistic has priority over the linguistic in such acts. The perlocutionary function is also the least communicable because it is less an intentional act, calling for an intention of recognition on the part of the hearer, than a kind of "stimulus" generating a "response" in a behavioral sense. The perlocutionary function helps us rather to identify the boundary between the act character and the reflex character of language.

The locutionary and illocutionary acts are acts — and therefore events — to the extent that their intention implies the intention of being recognized for what they are: a singular identification, universal predication, statement, order, wish, promise, etc.[4] This role of recognition allows us to say that the intention of saying is itself communicable to a certain extent. The intention does have a psychological aspect which is experienced as such only by the speaker. In the promise, for example, there is a commitment; in an assertion, a belief; in a wish, a want; etc., which constitute the psychological condition of the speech act, if we follow John Searle's analysis.[5] But these "mental acts" (Peter Geach) are not radically incommunicable. Their intention implies the intention of being recognized, therefore the intention of the other's intention. This intention of being identified, acknowledged, and recognized as such by the other is part of the intention itself. In the vocabulary of Husserl, we could say that it is the noetic in the psychic.

The criterion of the noetic is the intention of communicability, the expectation of recognition in the intentional act itself. The noetic is the soul of discourse as dialogue. The difference between the illocutionary and the perlocutionary, therefore, is nothing else than the presence in the former and the absence in the latter of the intention to produce in the listener a certain mental act by means of which he will recognize my intention.

This reciprocity of intentions is the event of dialogue. The bearer of this event is the "grammar" of recognition included in the intended meaning.

To conclude this discussion of the dialectic of event and meaning, we may say that language is itself the process by which private experience is made public. Language is the exteriorization thanks to which an impression is transcended and becomes an ex-pression, or, in other words, the transformation of the psychic into the noetic. Exteriorization and communicability are one and the same thing for they are nothing other than this elevation of a part of our life into the *logos* of discourse. There the solitude of life is for a moment, anyway, illuminated by the common light of discourse.

Meaning as "Sense" and "Reference"

In the two preceding sections the dialectic of event and meaning has been developed as an inner dialectic of the meaning of discourse. To mean is what the speaker does. But it is also what the sentence does. The utterance meaning—in the sense of the propositional content—is the "objective" side of this meaning. The utterer's meaning—in the threefold sense of the self-reference of the sentence, the illocutionary dimension of the speech act, and the intention of recognition by the hearer — is the "subjective" side of the meaning.

This subjective-objective dialectic does not exhaust the meaning of meaning and therefore does not exhaust the structure of discourse. The "objective" side of discourse itself may be taken in two different ways. We may mean the "what" of discourse or the "about what" of discourse. The "what" of discourse is its "sense," the "about what" is its "reference." This distinction between sense and reference was introduced into modern philosophy by Gottlob Frege in his famous article *"Ueber Sinn und Bedeutung,"* which has been translated into English as "On Sense and Reference."[6] It is a distinction which can be directly connected with our initial distinction

19

between semiotics and semantics. Only the sentence level allows us to distinguish what is said and about what it is said. In the system of language, say as a lexicon, there is no problem of reference; signs only refer to other signs within the system. With the sentence, however, language is directed beyond itself. Whereas the sense is immanent to the discourse, and objective in the sense of ideal, the reference expresses the movement in which language transcends itself. In other words, the sense correlates the identification function and the predicative function within the sentence, and the reference relates language to the world. It is another name for discourse's claim to be true.

The decisive fact here is that language has a reference only when it is used. As Strawson has shown in his famous response to Russell's article, "On Denoting," the same sentence, i.e., the same sense, may or may not refer depending on the circumstances or situation of an act of discourse.[7] No inner mark, independent of the use of a sentence, constitutes a reliable criterion of denotation. Consequently, the dialectic of sense and reference is not unrelated to the previous dialectic of event and meaning. To refer is what the sentence does in a certain situation and according to a certain use. It is also what the speaker does when he applies his words to reality. That someone refers to something at a certain time is an event, a speech event. But this event receives its structure from the meaning as sense. The speaker refers to something on the basis of, or through, the ideal structure of the sense. The sense, so to speak, is traversed by the referring intention of the speaker. In this way the dialectic of event and meaning receives a new development from the dialectic of sense and reference.

But the dialectic of sense and reference is so original that it can be taken as an independent guideline. Only this dialectic says something about the relation between language and the ontological condition of being in the world. Language is not a world of its own. It is not even a world. But because we are in the world, because we are affected by situations, and because we orient ourselves comprehensively in those situations, we have something to say, we have experience to bring to language.

This notion of bringing experience to language is the ontological condition of reference, an ontological condition reflected within language as a postulate which has not immanent justification; the postulate according to which we presuppose the existence of singular things which we identify. We presuppose that something must be in order that something may be identified. This postulation of existence as the ground of identification is what Frege ultimately meant when he said that we are not satisfied by the sense alone, but we presuppose a reference.[8] And this postulation is so necessary that we must add a specific prescription if we want to refer to fictional entities such as characters in a novel or a play. This additional rule of suspension confirms that the function of singular identification raises in an originary way a legitimate question of existence.

But this intentional pointing toward the extra-linguistic would rely on a mere postulate and would remain a questionable leap beyond language if this exteriorization were not the counterpart of a previous and more originary move starting from the experience of being in the world and proceeding from this ontological condition towards its expression in language. It is because there is first something to say, because we have an experience to bring to language, that conversely, language is not only directed towards ideal meanings but also refers to what is.

As I said, this dialectic is so fundamental and so originary that it could rule the whole theory of language as discourse and even provide a reformulation of the nuclear dialectic of event and meaning. If language were not fundamentally referential, would or could it be meaningful? How could we know that a sign stands for something, if it did not receive its direction towards something for which it stands from its use in discourse? Finally, semiotics appears as a mere abstraction of semantics. And the semiotic definition of the sign as an inner difference between signifier and signified presupposes its semantic definition as reference to the thing for which it stands. The most concrete definition of semantics, then, is the theory that relates the inner or immanent constitution of the sense to the outer or transcendent intention of the reference.

This universal signification of the problem of reference is so broad that even the utterer's meaning has to be expressed in the language of reference as the self-reference of discourse, i.e., as the designation of its speaker by the structure of discourse. Discourse refers back to its speaker at the same time that it refers to the world. This correlation is not fortuitous, since it is ultimately the speaker who refers to the world in speaking. Discourse in action and in use refers backwards and forwards, to a speaker and a world.

Such is the ultimate criterion of language as discourse.

Some Hermeneutical Implications

It is possible, even at this early stage of our inquiry, to anticipate some of the implications of the preceding analysis for our interpretation theory.

They mainly concern the use and abuse of the concept of speech event in the Romanticist tradition of hermeneutics. Hermeneutics as issuing from Schleiermacher and Dilthey tended to identify interpretation with the category of "understanding," and to define understanding as the recognition of an author's intention from the point of view of the primitive addressees in the original situation of discourse. This priority given to the author's intention and to the original audience tended, in turn, to make dialogue the model of every situation of understanding, thereby imposing the framework of inter-subjectivity on hermeneutics. Understanding a text, then, is only a particular case of the dialogical situation in which someone responds to someone else.

This psychologizing conception of hermeneutics has had a great influence on Christian theology. It nourished the theologies of the Word-Event for which the event par excellence is a speech event, and this speech event is the Kerygma, the preaching of the Gospel. The meaning of the original event testifies to itself in the present event by which we apply it to ourselves in the act of faith.

My attempt here is to call into question the assumptions of this hermeneutic from the point of view of a philosophy of discourse in order to release hermeneutics from its psychologizing and existential prejudices. But my purpose is not to oppose to this hermeneutic based on the category of the speech event a hermeneutic which would merely be its opposite, as would be a structural analysis of the propositional content of texts. Such a hermeneutic would suffer from the same non-dialogical onesidedness. The assumptions of a psychologizing hermeneutic — like those of its contrary hermeneutic — stem from a double misunderstanding of the dialectic of event and meaning in discourse and the dialectic of sense and reference in meaning itself. This twofold misunderstanding in turn leads to assigning an erroneous task to interpretion, a task which is well expressed in the famous slogan, "to understand an author better than he understood himself." Therefore what is at stake in this discussion is the correct definition of the hermeneutical task.

I do not claim that the present essay suffices by itself to eliminate all misunderstanding. Without a specific investigation of writing, a theory of discourse is not yet a theory of the text. But if we succeed in showing that a written text is a form of discourse, discourse under the condition of inscription, then the conditions of the possibility of discourse are also those of the text. As our discussion of these conditions has shown, the notion of the speech event is not cancelled, rather it is submitted to a series of dialectical polarities summarized under the double title of event and meaning and sense and reference. These dialectical polarities allow us to anticipate that the concepts of intention and dialogue are not to be excluded from hermeneutics, but instead are to be released from the onesidedness of a non-dialectical concept of discourse.

It is in this way that the present essay is, if not the kernel of the whole series, truly the *initial* essay in the strong sense of the word.

2.

SPEAKING AND WRITING

To the extent that hermeneutics is text-oriented interpretation, and inasmuch as texts are, among other things, instances of written language, no interpretation theory is possible that does not come to grips with the problem of writing. The purpose of this essay therefore is twofold. I want first to show that the transition from speaking to writing has its conditions of possibility in the theory of discourse described in the first essay, especially in the dialectic of event and meaning considered there. My second purpose is to connect the kind of intentional exteriorization that writing exhibits with a central problem of hermeneutics, that of distanciation. This same concept of exteriority, which in the first part of this essay will be more used than criticized, will become problematic in the second part. Plato's critique of writing as a kind of alienation will provide the turning point from the descriptive to the critical treatment of the exteriorization of discourse proper to writing.

From Speaking to Writing

What happens in writing is the full manifestation of something that is in a virtual state, something nascent and inchoate, in living speech, namely the detachment of meaning from the event. But this detachment is not such as to cancel the fundamental structure of discourse discussed in my first essay. The semantic autonomy of the text which now appears is still governed by the dialectic of event and meaning. Moreover, it may be said that this dialectic is made obvious and explicit by writing. Writing is the full manifestation of discourse. To hold, as Jacques Derrida does,[1] that writing has a root distinct from speech and that this foundation has been misunderstood due to our having paid excessive attention to speech, its voice, and its *logos*, is to overlook the grounding of both modes of the actualization of discourse in the dialectical constitution of discourse.

I propose instead that we begin from the schema of communication described by Roman Jakobson in his famous article, "Linguistics and Poetics."[2] To the six main "factors" of communicative discourse — the speaker, hearer, medium or channel, code, situation, and message—he relates six correlative "functions": the emotive, conative, phatic, metalinguistic, referential, and poetic functions. Taking this schema as a starting point, we may inquire into what alterations, transformations, or deformations affect the interplay of facts and functions when discourse is inscribed in writing.

Message and Medium: Fixation

The most obvious change from speaking to writing concerns the relation between the message and its medium or channel. At first glance, it concerns only this relation, but upon closer examination, the first alteration irradiates in every direction, affecting in a decisive manner all the factors and functions. Our task, therefore, will be to proceed from this central change toward its various peripheral effects.

As a simple change in the nature of the medium of communication, the problem of writing is identical to that of the fixation of discourse in some exterior bearer, whether it be stone, papyrus, or paper, which is other than the human voice. This inscription, substituted for the immediate vocal, physiognomic, or gestural expression, is in itself a tremendous cultural achievement. The human fact disappears. Now material "marks" convey the message. This cultural achievement concerns the event character of discourse first and subsequently the meaning as well. It is because discourse only exists in a temporal and present instance of discourse that it may flee as speech or be fixed as writing. Because the event appears and disappears, there is a problem of fixation, of inscription. What we want to fix is discourse, not language as *langue*. It is only by extension that we fix by inscription the alphabet, the lexicon, and the grammar, all of which serve that which alone is to be fixed: discourse. The atemporal system of language neither appears or disappears, it simply does not happen. Only discourse is to be fixed, because discourse as event disappears.

But this nondialectical description of the phenomenon of fixation does not reach the core of the process of inscription. Writing may rescue the instance of discourse because what writing actually does fix is not the event of speaking but the "said" of speaking, i.e., the intentional exteriorization constitutive of the couple "event-meaning." What we write, what we inscribe is the noema of the act of speaking, the meaning of the speech event, not the event as event. This inscription, in spite of the perils that we shall later evoke following Plato in the second part of this essay, is discourse's destination. Only when the *sagen* — the "saying" — has become *Aus-sage*, e-nunciation, only then, is discourse accomplished as discourse in the full expression of its nuclear dialectic.

It is not necessary here that we consider at length the notion of the speech event in terms of its complete description as a speech act, i.e., as a locutionary, illocutionary, and perlocutionary act. As I have shown in my first essay, each of these acts gives way to the dialectic of event and meaning. Thanks to the grammatical marks which express it in an exterior and public way, the intentional exteriorization of discourse concerns the whole hierarchy of partial speech acts. The locutionary act exteriorizes itself in the sentence, the inner structure of which may be identified and re-identified as being the same, and which, therefore, may be inscribed and preserved. To the extent that the illocutionary act can be exteriorized thanks to grammatical paradigms and procedures expressive of its "force," it too can be inscribed. But to the extent that in spoken discourse the illocutionary force depends upon mimicry and gesture, and upon the nonarticulated aspects of discourse, which we call prosody, it must be acknowledged that the illocutionary force is less inscribable than the propositional meaning. Finally, the perlocutionary act is the least inscribable aspect of discourse for the reasons

27

given in the previous essay. It characterizes spoken language more than it does written language.

In all cases it is the intentional exteriorization proper to the different layers of the speech act that makes inscription in writing possible, so that in the final analysis the extension of the problematics of fixation is equal to that of the intentional exteriorization of the speech act with its multidimensional structure.

Now, does the problematics of fixation and inscription exhaust the problem of writing?

In other words, is writing only a question of a change of medium, where the human voice, face, and gesture are replaced by material marks other than the speaker's own body?

When we consider the range of social and political changes which can be related to the invention of writing, we may surmise that writing is much more than mere material fixation. We need only remind ourselves of some of these tremendous achievements. To the possibility of transferring orders over long distances without serious distortions may be connected the birth of political rule exercised by a distant state. This political implication of writing is just one of its consequences. To the fixation of rules for reckoning may be referred the birth of market relationships, therefore the birth of economics. To the constitution of archives, history. To the fixation of law as a standard of decisions, independent from the opinion of the concrete judge, the birth of the justice and juridical codes, etc. Such an immense range of effects suggests that human discourse is not merely preserved from destruction by being fixed in writing, but that it is deeply affected in its communicative function.

A second consideration may encourage us to pursue this new thought. Writing raises a specific problem as soon as it is not merely the fixation of a previous oral discourse, the inscription of spoken language, but is human thought directly brought to writing without the intermediary stage of spoken language. Then writing takes the place of speaking. A kind of short-cut occurs between the meaning of discourse and the material medium. Then we have to do with literature in the

28

original sense of the word. The fate of discourse is delivered over to *littera*, not to *vox*.

The best way to measure the extent of this substitution is to look at the range of changes which occur among the other components of the communication process.

Message and Speaker

The first connection to be altered is that of the message to the speaker. This change indeed is itself one of two symmetrical changes, which affect the interlocutionary situation as a whole. The relation between message and speaker at one end of the communication chain and the relation between message and hearer at the other are together deeply transformed when the face-to-face relation is replaced by the more complex relation of reading to writing, resulting from the direct inscription of discourse in *littera*. The dialogical situation has been exploded. The relation writing-reading is no longer a particular case of the relation speaking-hearing.

If we consider these changes in more detail we see that the reference of the discourse back to its speaker is affected in the following way. In discourse, we said, the sentence designates its speaker by diverse indicators of subjectivity and personality. But in spoken discourse this ability of discourse to refer back to the speaking subject presents a character of immediacy because the speaker belongs to the situation of interlocution. He is there, in the genuine sense of being-there, of *Da-sein*. Consequently the subjective intention of the speaker and the discourse's meaning overlap each other in such a way that it is the same thing to understand what the speaker means and what his discourse means. The ambiguity of the German *meinen* and the English "to mean" — which we examined in the preceding essay—attests to this overlapping in the dialogical situation. With written discourse, however, the author's intention and the meaning of the text cease to coincide. This dissociation of the verbal meaning of the text and the mental intention of the author gives to the concept of inscription its decisive significance, beyond the mere fixation of previous oral discourse. Inscription becomes synonymous with the semantic autonomy of the text, which results from the discon-

29

nection of the mental intention of the author from the verbal meaning of the text, of what the author meant and what the text means. The text's career escapes the finite horizon lived by its author. What the text means now matters more than what the author meant when he wrote it.

This concept of semantic autonomy is of tremendous importance for hermeneutics. Exegesis begins with it, i.e., it unfolds its procedures within the circumscription of a set of meanings that have broken their moorings to the psychology of the author. But this de-psychologizing of interpretation does not imply that the notion of authorial meaning has lost all significance. Here again a non-dialectical conception of the relation between event and meaning would tend to oppose one alternative to the other. On the one hand, we would have what W. K. Wimsatt calls the intentional fallacy, which holds the author's intention as the criterion for any valid interpretation of the text, and, on the other hand, what I would call in a symmetrical fashion the fallacy of the absolute text: the fallacy of hypostasizing the text as an authorless entity. If the intentional fallacy overlooks the semantic autonomy of the text, the opposite fallacy forgets that a text remains a discourse told by somebody, said by someone to someone else about something. It is impossible to cancel out this main characteristic of discourse without reducing texts to natural objects, i.e., to things which are not man-made, but which, like pebbles, are found in the sand.

The semantic autonomy of the text makes the relation of event and meaning more complex and in this sense reveals it as a dialectical relation. The authorial meaning becomes properly a dimension of the text to the extent that the author is not available for questioning. When the text no longer answers, then it has an author and no longer a speaker. The authorial meaning is the dialectical counterpart of the verbal meaning, and they have to be construed in terms of each other. These concepts of author and authorial meaning raise a hermeneutical problem contemporaneous with that of semantic autonomy.

Message and Hearer

At the opposite end of the communication chain the relation of the textual message to the reader is no less complex than is the relation to the author. Whereas spoken discourse is addressed to someone who is determined in advanced by the dialogical situation—it is addressed to you, the second person — a written text is addressed to an unknown reader and potentially to whoever knows how to read. This universaliziaton of the audience is one of the more striking effects of writing and may be expressed in terms of a paradox. Because discourse is now linked to a material support, it becomes more spiritual in the sense that it is liberated from the narrowness of the face-to-face situation.

Of course this universality is only potential. In fact, a book is addressed to only a section of the public and reaches its appropriate readers through media that are themselves submitted to social rules of exclusion and admission. In other words, reading is a social phenomenon, which obeys certain patterns and therefore suffers from specific limitations. Nevertheless, the proposition which says that a text is potentially addressed to whoever knows how to read must be retained as a limit on any sociology of reading. A work also creates its public. In this way it enlarges the circle of communication and properly initates new modes of communication. To that extent, the recognition of the work by the audience created by the work is an unpredictable event.

Once again the dialectic of meaning and event is exhibited in its fullness by writing. Discourse is revealed as discourse by the dialectic of the address, which is both universal and contingent. On the one hand, it is the semantic autonomy of the text which opens up the range of potential readers and, so to speak, creates the audience of the text. On the other hand, it is the response of the audience which makes the text important and therefore significant. This is why authors who do not worry about their readers and despise their present public keep speaking of their readers as a secret community, sometimes projected into a cloudy future. It is part of the meaning of a text to be open to an indefinite number of readers and,

31

therefore, of interpretations. This opportunity for multiple readings is the dialectical counterpart of the semantic autonomy of the text.

It follows that the problem of the appropriation of the meaning of the text becomes as paradoxical as that of the authorship. The right of the reader and the right of the text converge in an important struggle that generates the whole dynamic of interpretation. Hermeneutics begins where dialogue ends.

Message and Code

The relation between message and code is made more complex by writing in a somewhat indirect way. What I have in mind here concerns the function of literary genres in the production of discourse as such and such a mode of discourse, whether poem, narrative, or essay. This function undoubtedly concerns the relation between message and code since genres are generative devices to produce discourse as. . . . Before being classificatory devices used by literary critics to orient themselves in the profusion of literary works, therefore before being artifacts of criticism, they are to discourse what generative grammar is to the grammaticality of individual sentences. In this sense, these discursive codes may be joined those phonological, lexical, and syntactical codes which rule the units of discourse, sentences. Now the question is to what extent literary genres are genuinely codes of writing? Only in an indirect, but nevertheless decisive way.

Literary genres display some conditions which theoretically could be described without considering writing. The function of these generative devices is to produce new entities of language longer than the sentence, organic wholes irreducible to a mere addition of sentences. A poem, narrative, or essay relies on laws of composition which in principle are indifferent to the opposition between speaking and writing. They proceed from the application of dynamic forms to sets of sentences for which the difference between oral and written language is unessential. Instead, the specificity of these dynamic forms seems to proceed from another dichotomy than that of speaking and hearing, from the application to discourse of categories borrowed from another field, that of practice and work. Language is submitted to the rules of a kind of craftsmanship, which allows us to speak of production and of works of art, and, by extension of works of discourse. Poems, narratives, and essays are such works of discourse. The generative devices, which we call literary genres, are the technical rules presiding over their production. And the style of a work is nothing else than the individual configuration of a singular product or work. The author here is not only the speaker, but also the maker of this work, which is his work.

But, if the dichotomy between theory and practice is irreducible to the pair speaking-writing, writing plays a decisive role precisely in the application of the categories of practice, technique, and work to discourse. There is production when a form is applied to some matter in order to shape it. When discourse is transferred to the field of production it is also treated as a stuff to be shaped. It is here that writing interferes. Inscription as a material support, the semantic autonomy of the text as regards both the speaker and the hearer, and all the related traits of exteriority characteristic of writing help to make language the matter of a specific craftsmanship. Thanks to writing, the works of language become as self-contained as sculptures. It is not by chance that "literature" designates both the status of language as written (*littera*) and as embodied in works according to literary genres. With literature the problems of inscription and production tend to overlap. The same may be said for the concept of text, which combines the condition of inscription with the texture proper to the works generated by the productive rules of literary composition. Text means discourse both as inscribed and wrought.

Such is the specific affinity that reigns between writing and the specific codes which generate the works of discourse. This affinity is so close that we might be tempted to say that even oral expressions of poetic or narrative compositions rely on processes equivalent to writing. The memorization of epic poems, lyrical songs, parables and proverbs, and their ritual recitation tend to fix and even to freeze the form of the work in such a way that memory appears as the support of an inscription similar to that provided by external marks. In this ex-

33

tended sense of inscription, writing and the production of works of discourse according to the rules of literary composition tend to coincide without being identical processes.

Message and Reference

I have postponed considering the most complex changes that occur in the functioning of discourse, which may be ascribed to writing, until the end of this inquiry. They concern the referential function of discourse in the schema of communication proposed by Roman Jakobson, and they are the most complex effects for two reasons. On the one hand, the distinction between sense and reference introduces in discourse a more complex dialectic than that of event and meaning, which provides us with the model of exteriorization that makes writing possible. It is, so to speak, a dialectic of the second order where the meaning itself, as immanent "sense," is externalized as transcendent reference, in the sense that thought is directed through the sense towards different kinds of extralinguistic entities such as objects, states of affairs, things, facts, etc. On the other hand, most of the alterations of reference which will be considered are not to be ascribed to writing as such but to writing as the ordinary mediation of the modes of discourse which constitute literature. Some of these alterations are even directly produced by the strategy proper to specific literary genres such as poetry. Inscription, then, is only indirectly responsible for the new fate of reference.

Yet despite these reservations, the following may be said: in spoken discourse the ultimate criterion for the referential scope of what we say is the possibility of showing the thing referred to as a member of the situation common to both speaker and hearer. This situation surrounds the dialogue, and its landmarks can all be shown by a gesture or by pointing a finger. Or it can be designated in an ostensive manner by the discourse itself through the oblique reference of those indicators which include the demonstratives, the adverbs of time and place, and the tenses of the verb. Finally they can be described in such a definite way that one, and only one, thing may be identified within the common framework of reference. Indeed, the ostensive indicators and, still more, the

34

definite descriptions work in the same way in both oral and written discourse. They provide singular identifications, and singular identifications need not rely on showing in the sense of a gestural indication of the thing referred to. Nevertheless singular identifications ultimately refer to the here and now determined by the interlocutionary situation. There is no identification which does not relate that about which we speak to a unique position in the spatio-temporal network, and there is no network of places in time and space without a final reference to the situational here and now. In this ultimate sense, all references of oral language rely on monstrations, which depend on the situation perceived as common by the members of the dialogue. All references in the dialogical situation consequently are situational.

It is this grounding of reference in the dialogical situation that is shattered by writing. Ostensive indicators and definite descriptions continue to identify singular entities, but a gap appears between identification and monstration. The absence of a common situation generated by the spatial and temporal distance between writer and reader; the cancellation of the absolute here and now by the substitution of material external marks for the voice, face, and body of the speaker as the absolute origin of all the places in space and time; and the semantic autonomy of the text, which severs it from the present of the writer and opens it to an indefinite range of potential readers in an indeterminate time—all these alterations of the temporal constitution of discourse are reflected in parallel alterations of the ostensive character of the reference.

Some texts merely restructure for their readers the conditions of ostensive reference. Letters, travel reports, geographical descriptions, diaries, historical monographs, and in general all descriptive accounts of reality may provide the reader with an equivalent of ostensive reference in the mode of "as if" ("as if you were there"), thanks to the ordinary procedures of singular identification. The heres and theres of the text may be tacitly referred to the absolute here and there of the reader, thanks to the unique spatio-temporal network to which both writer and reader ultimately belong and which they both acknowledge.

This first extension of the scope of reference beyond the narrow boundaries of the dialogical situation is of tremendous consequence. Thanks to writing, man and only man has a world and not just a situation. This extension is one more example of the spiritual implications of the substitution of material marks for the bodily support of oral discourse. In the same manner that the text frees its meaning from the tutelage of the mental intention, it frees its reference from the limits of situational reference. For us, the world is the ensemble of references opened up by the texts, or, at least for the moment, by descriptive texts. It is in this way that we may speak of the Greek "world," which is not to imagine anymore what were the situations for those who lived there, but to designate the nonsituational references displayed by the descriptive accounts of reality.

A second extension of the scope of reference is much more difficult to interpret. It proceeds less from writing as such as from the open or covert strategy of certain modes of discourse. Therefore it concerns literature more than writing, or writing as the channel of literature. In the construction of his schema of communication, Roman Jakobson relates the poetic function — which is to be understood in a broader sense than just poetry—to the emphasis of the message for its own sake at the expense of the reference. We have already anticipated this eclipsing of the reference by comparing poetic discourse to a self-contained sculptural work. The gap between situational and non-situational reference, implied in the "as if" reference of descriptive accounts, is now unbridgeable. This can be seen in fictional narratives, i.e., in narratives that are not descriptive reports where a narrative time, expressed by specific tenses of the verbs, is displayed by and within the narrative without any connection to the unique space-time network common to ostensive and non-ostensive discription.

Does this mean that this eclipse of reference, in either the ostensive or descriptive sense, amounts to a sheer abolition of all reference? No. My contention is that discourse cannot fail to be about something. In saying this, I am denying the ideology of absolute texts. Only a few sophisticated texts, along the line of Mallarmé's poetry, satisfy this ideal of a text without reference. But this modern kind of literature stands as a limiting case and an exception. It cannot give the key to all other texts, even poetic texts, in Jakobson's sense, which include all fictional literature whether lyrical or narrative. In one manner or another, poetic texts speak about the world. But not in a descriptive way. As Jakobson himself suggests, the reference here is not abolished, but divided or split. The effacement of the ostensive and descriptive reference liberates a power of reference to aspects of our being in the world that cannot be said in a direct descriptive way, but only alluded to, thanks to the referential values of metaphoric and, in general, symbolic expressions.

We ought to enlarge our concept of the world, therefore, not only to allow for non-ostensive but still descriptive references, but also non-ostensive and non-descriptive references, those of poetic diction. The term "world" then has the meaning that we all understand when we say of a new born child that he has come into the world. For me, the world is the ensemble of references opened up by every kind of text, descriptive or poetic, that I have read, understood, and loved. And to understand a text is to interpolate among the predicates of our situation all the significations that make a *Welt* out of our *Umwelt*. It is this enlarging of our horizon of existence that permits us to speak of the references opened up by the text or of the world opened up by the referential claims of most texts.

In this sense, Heidegger rightly says, in his analysis of *Verstehen* in *Being and Time*,[3] that what we understand first in a discourse is not another person, but a "pro-ject," that is, the outline of a new way of being in the world. Only writing — given the two reservations made at the beginning of this section—in freeing itself, not only from its author and from its originary audience, but from the narrowness of the dialogical situation, reveals this destination of discourse as projecting a world.

A Plea for Writing

The preceding analysis has reached its goal. It has shown the full manifestation of the nuclear dialectic of event and meaning, and of the intentional exteriorization already at work in oral discourse, although in an inchoative way. But by pushing it to the forefront it has made problematic what could be taken for granted as long as it remained implicit. Is not this intentional exteriorization delivered over to material marks a kind of alienation?

This question is so radical that it requires that we assume in the most positive way the condition of exteriority, not only as a cultural accident, as a contingent condition for discourse and thought, but as a necessary conditon of the hermeneutical process. Only a hermeneutic using distanciation in a productive way may solve the paradox of the intentional exteriorization of discourse.

Against Writing

The attack against writing comes from afar. It is linked to a certain model of knowledge, science, and wisdom used by Plato to condemn exteriority as being contrary to genuine reminiscence.[4] He presents it in the form of a myth because philosophy here has to do with the coming to being of an institution, a skill, and a power, lost in the dark past of culture and connected with Egypt, the cradle of religious wisdom. The king of Thebes receives in his city the god Theuth, who has invented numbers, geometry, astronomy, games of chance, and *grammata* or written characters. Questioned about the powers and possible benefits of his invention, Theuth claims that the knowledge of written characters would make Egyptians wiser and more capable of preserving the memory of things. No, replies the king, souls will become more forgetful once they have put their confidence in external marks instead of relying on themselves from within. This "remedy" (*pharmakon*) is not reminiscence, but sheer re-memoration. As to instruction, what this invention brings is not the reality, but the resemblance of it; not wisdom, but its appearance.

The commentary of Socrates is no less interesting. Writing is like painting which generates non-living being, which in turn remains silent when asked to answer. Writings, too, if one questions them in order to learn from them, "signify a unique thing always the same." Besides this sterile sameness, writings are indifferent to their addressees. Wandering here and there, they are heedless of whom they reach. And if a dispute arises, or if they are injustly despised, they still need the help of their father. By themselves they are unable to rescue themselves.

According to this harsh critique, as the apology for true reminiscence, the principle and soul of right and genuine discourse, discourse accompanied with wisdom (or science), is written in the soul of the one who knows, the one who is able to defend himself, and keep silent or talk as required by the soul of the person addressed.

This Platonic attack against writing is not an isolated example in the history of our culture. Rousseau and Bergson, for example, for different reasons link the main evils that plague civilization to writing. For Rousseau, as long as language relied only on the voice, it preserved the presence of oneself to oneself and to others. Language was still the expression of passion. It was eloquence, not yet exegesis. With writing began separation, tyranny, and inequality. Writing ignores its addressee just as it conceals its author. It separates men just as property separates owners. The tyranny of the lexicon and of grammar is equal to that of the laws of exchange, crystallized in money. Instead of the Word of God, we have the rule of the learned and the domination of the priesthood. The break-up of the speaking community, the partition of the soil, the analycity of thought, and the reign of dogmaticism were all born with writing.

An echo of Platonic reminiscence may, therefore, still be heard in this apology for the voice as the bearer of one's presence to oneself and as the inner link of a community without distance.

Bergson directly questions the principle of exteriority, which witnesses to the infiltration of space into the temporality of sound and its continuity. The genuine word emerges from the "intellectual effort" to fulfill a previous intention of saying, in the search for the appropriate expression. The written word, as the deposit of this search, has severed its ties with the feeling, effort, and dynamism of thought. The breath, song, and rhythm are over and the figure takes their place. It captures and fascinates. It scatters and isolates. This is why the authentic creators such as Socrates and Jesus have left no writings, and why the genuine mystics renounce statements and articulated thought.

Once more the interiority of the phonic effort is opposed to the exteriority of dead imprints which are unable to "rescue" themselves.

Writing and Iconicity

The rejoinder to such critiques must be as radical as the challenge. It is no longer possible to rely on just a description of the movement from speaking to writing. The critique summons us to legitimate what has been hitherto simply taken for granted.

A remark made in passing in the *Phaedrus* provides us with an important clue. Writing is compared to painting, the images of which are said to be weaker and less real than living beings. The question here is whether the theory of the *eikon*, which is held to be a mere shadow of reality, is not the presupposition of every critique addressed to any mediation through exterior marks..

If it could be shown that painting is not this shadowy reduplication of reality, then it would be possible to return to the problem of writing as a chapter in a general theory of iconicity, such as François Dagognet elaborates in his book, *Ecriture et Iconographie*.[5]

Far from yielding less than the original, pictorial activity may be characterized in terms of an "iconic augmentation," where the strategy of painting, for example, is to reconstruct reality on the basis of a limited optic alphabet. This strategy of contraction and miniaturization yields more by handling less. In this way, the main effect of painting is to resist the entropic tendency of ordinary vision — the shadow image of Plato —

and to increase the meaning of the universe by capturing it in the network of its abbreviated signs. This effect of saturation and culmination, within the tiny space of the frame and on the surface of a two-dimensional canvas, in opposition to the optical erosion proper to ordinary vision, is what is meant by iconic augmentation. Whereas in ordinary vision qualities tend to neutralize one another, to blur their edges, and to shade off their contrasts, painting, at least since the invention of oil painting by Dutch artists, enhances the contrasts, gives colors back their resonance, and lets appear the luminoisity within which things shine. The history of the techniques of painting teaches us that these meaningful effects followed upon the material invention of pigments made active by being mixed with oil. This selection of what I just called the optic alphabet of the painter allowed him to preserve the colors from diluting and tarnishing and to incorporate into his pictures the deep refraction of light beneath the mere reflective effect of surface luminosity.

Because the painter could master a new alphabetic material —because he was a chemist, distillator, varnisher, and glazer —he was able to write a new text of reality. Painting for the Dutch masters was neither the reproduction nor the production of the universe, but its metamorphosis.

In this respect, the techniques of engraving and etching are equally instructive. Whereas photography—at least unskilled photography — grasps everything but holds nothing, the magic of engraving, celebrated by Baudelaire, may exhibit the essential. This is because engraving, as with painting, although with other means, relies on the invention of an alphabet, i.e., a set of minimal signs, consisting of syncope points, strokes, and white patches, which enhance the trait and surround it with absence.

Impressionism and abstract art, as well, proceed more and more boldly to the abolition of natural forms for the sake of a merely constructed range of elementary signs whose combinatory forms will rival ordinary vision. With abstract art, painting is close to science in that it challenges perceptual forms by relating them to non-perceptual structures. The graphic capture of the universe, here too, is served by a radical

41

denial of the immediate. Painting seems only to "produce," no longer to "reproduce." But it catches up with reality at the level of its elements, as does the God of the *Timaeus*. Constructivism is only the boundary case of a process of augmentation where the apparent denial of reality is the condition for the glorification of the non-figurative essence of things. Iconicity, then, means the revelation of a real more real than ordinary reality.

This theory of iconicity — as aesthetic augmentation of reality — gives us the key to a decisive answer to Plato's critique of writing. Iconicity is the re-writing of reality. Writing, in the limited sense of the word, is a particular case of iconicity. The inscription of discourse is the transcription of the world, and transcription is not reduplication, but metamorphosis.

This positive value of the material mediation by written signs may be ascribed, in writing as in painting, to the invention of notational systems presenting analytical properties: discreteness, finite number, combinatory power. The triumph of the phonetic alphabet in Western cultures and the apparent subordination of writing to speaking stemming from the dependence of letters on sounds, however, must not let us forget the other possibilities of inscription expressed by pictograms, hieroglyphs, and above all, by ideograms, which represent a direct inscription of thought meanings and which can be read differently in different idioms. These other kinds of inscription exhibit a universal character of writing, equally present in phonetic writing, but which the dependence on sounds there tends to dissimulate: the space-structure not only of the bearer, but of the marks, themselves, of their form, position, mutual distance, order, and linear disposition. The transfer from hearing to reading is fundamentally linked to this transfer from the temporal properties of the voice to the spatial properties of the inscribed marks. This general spatialization of language is complete with the appearance of printing. The visualization of culture begins with the dispossession of the power of the voice in the proximity of mutual presence. Printed texts reach man in solitude, far from the ceremonies that gather the community. Abstract relations, telecommunications in the proper sense of the word, connect the scattered members of an invisible public.

Such are the material instruments of the iconicity of writing and the transcription of reality through the external inscription of discourse.

Inscription and Productive Distanciation

We are now prepared for a final step. It will lead us to find in the process of interpretation itself the ultimate justification of the exteriorization of discourse.

The problem of writing becomes a hermeneutical problem when it is referred to its complementary pole, which is reading. A new dialectic then emerges, that of distanciation and appropriation. By appropriation I mean the counterpart of the semantic autonomy, which detached the text from its writer. To appropriate is to make "one's own" what was "alien." Because there is a general need for making our own what is foreign to us, there is a general problem of distanciation. Distance, then, is not simply a fact, a given, just the actual spatial and temporal gap between us and the appearance of such and such work of art or discourse. It is a dialectical trait, the principle of a struggle between the otherness that transforms all spatial and temporal distance into cultural estrangement and the ownness by which all understanding aims at the extension of self-understanding. Distanciation is not a quantitative phenomenon; it is the dynamic counterpart of our need, our interest, and our effort to overcome cultural estrangement. Writing and reading take place in this cultural struggle. Reading is the *pharmakon*, the "remedy," by which the meaning of the text is "rescued" from the estrangement of distanciation and put in a new proximity, a proximity which suppresses and preserves the cultural distance and includes the otherness within the ownness.

This general problematic is deeply rooted both in the history of thought and in our ontological situation.

Historically speaking, the problem which I am elaborating is the reformulation of a problem to which the eighteenth

43

century Enlightenment gave its first modern formulation for the sake of classical philology: how to make once more present the culture of antiquity in spite of the intervening cultural distance? German Romanticism gave a dramatic turn to this problem by asking how we can become contemporaneous with past geniuses? More generally, how is one to use the expressions of life fixed by writing in order to transfer oneself into a foreign psychic life? The problem returned again after the collapse of the Hegelian claim to overcome historicism by the logic of the Absolute Spirit. If there is no recapitulation of past cultural heritages in an all encompassing whole delivered from the onesidedness of its partial components, then the historicity of the transmission and reception of these heritages cannot be overcome. Then the dialectic of distanciation and appropriation is the last word in the absence of absolute knowledge.

This dialectic may also be expressed as that of the tradition as such, understood as the reception of historically transmitted cultural heritages. A tradition raises no philosophical problem as long as we live and dwell within it in the naiveté of the first certainty. Tradition only becomes problematic when this first naiveté is lost. Then we have to retrieve its meaning through and beyond estrangement. Henceforth the appropriation of the past proceeds along an endless struggle with distanciation. Interpretation, philosophically understood, is nothing else than an attempt to make estrangement and distanciation productive.[6]

Placed against the background of the dialectic of distanciation and appropriation, the relation between writing and reading accedes to its most fundamental meaning. At the same time, the partial dialectical processes, separately described in the opening section of this essay, following Jakobson's model of communication, make sense as a whole.

It will be the task of a discussion applied to the controversial concepts of explanation and understanding to grasp as a whole the paradoxes of authorial meaning and semantic autonomy, the personal addressee and the universal audience, the singular message and the typical literary codes, and the immanent structure and the world displayed by the text; a discussion I shall undertake in my fourth essay.

3.

METAPHOR AND SYMBOL
Translated by David Pellauer

This third essay is intercalated between the closing words of the preceding essay and the decisive discussion of the concepts of explanation and understanding in the following one for two specific reasons, both of which concern the extension of the field of the theory of interpretation.

The first reason concerns the functioning of the signification in works of literature as opposed to scientific works, whose significations are to be taken literally. The question here is whether the surplus of meaning characteristic of literary works is a part of their signification or if it must be understood as an external factor, which is noncognitive and simply emotional. I will consider metaphor as the touchstone of the cognitive value of literary works in the remarks which follow. If we can incorporate the surplus of meaning of metaphors into the domain of semantics, then we will be able to give the theory of verbal signification its greatest possible extension.

But is the verbal signification the whole signification? Is there not a surplus of meaning which goes beyond the linguistic sign? In my earlier writings, especially *The Symbolism of Evil* and *Freud and Philosophy*,[1] I directly defined hermeneutics by an object which seemed to be both as broad and as precise as possible, I mean the symbol. As regards the symbol, I defined it in turn by its semantic structure of having a double-meaning. Today I am less certain that one can attack the problem so directly without first having taken linguistics into account. Within the symbol, it now seems to me, there is something non-semantic as well as something semantic, and I will attempt to justify this assertion at the beginning of the second part of this essay. But assuming for the moment that I am correct, it follows that a better hypothesis would be to approach the symbol in terms of a structure of double-meaning, which is not a purely semantic structure, which, as we shall see, is the case with metaphor. But if the theory of metaphor can serve as a preparatory analysis leading up to the theory of the symbol, in return the theory of the symbol will allow us to extend our theory of signification by allowing us to include within it, not only verbal double-meaning, but non-verbal double-meaning as well. Thus metaphor and symbol will serve to mark out the field of extension for the theory of interpretation to be discussed in my concluding essay.

The Theory of Metaphor

Metaphor, says Monroe Beardsley, is "a poem in minia-ture."[2] Hence the relation between the literal meaning and the figurative meaning in a metaphor is like an abridged version within a single sentence of the complex interplay of significa-tions that characterize the literary work as a whole. Here by a literary work I mean a work of discourse distinguished from every other work of discourse, especially scientific discourse, in that it brings an explicit and an implicit meaning into relation.

The first question to be considered deals with the cognitive status of these two meanings. Within the tradition of logical positivism this distinction between explicit and implicit meaning was treated as the distinction between cognitive and emotive language. And a good part of literary criticism influ-enced by this positivist tradition transposed the distinction between cognitive and emotive language into the vocabulary of denotation and connotation. For such a position only the denotation is cognitive and, as such, is of a semantic order. A connotation is extra-semantic because it consists of the weav-ing together of emotive evocations, which lack cognitive value. The figurative sense of a text, therefore, must be seen as being bereft of any cognitive significance. But is this limita-tion of cognitive significance to just the denotative aspects of a sentence correct?

Such is the problem for which metaphor may function as a test case. If we can show that the relation between the literal and figurative meaning in a metaphor is a relation internal to the overall signification of the metaphor, we will thereby obtain a model for a purely semantic definition of literature, which will be applicable to each of its three essential classes: poetry, essays, and prose fiction. We can then say that what a poem states is related to what it suggests just as its primary signification is related to its secondary signification where both significations fall within the semantic field. And literature is that use of discourse where several things are specified at the same time and where the reader is not required to choose among them. It is the positive and productive use of ambiguity.

If we abstract for the moment from the world of the work revealed by this interplay of meanings, we may concentrate our analysis on the verbal design, i.e., the work of discourse, which generates the semantic ambiguity that characterizes a literary work. It is this work of discourse that can be seen in miniature in metaphor.

The theory of metaphor comes down to us from the ancient rhetoricians, but this theory will not fulfill the role we expect of it without one important revision. This revision, briefly stated, shifts the problem of metaphor from the semantics of the word to the semantics of the sentence.

In traditional rhetoric metaphor is classed as a trope, i.e., as one of the figures which classify the variations in meaning in the use of words and, more precisely, in the process of denomination. Metaphor belongs to the language game which governs naming. Thus we read in Aristotle's *Poetics* that a metaphor is "the application to a thing of a name that belongs to something else, the transference taking place from genus to species, from species to genus, from species to species, or proportionally."[3] His *Rhetoric* takes this definition for granted, simply adding a marginal note concerning the use of comparative images, which are characterized as a special form of the proportional metaphor in which the comparison is explicitly marked by a comparative term such as "is like . . ." Comparison, in other words, is an expanded form of metaphor. Cicero and Quintilian later inverted this model and said that a metaphor is simply an abridged comparison.

Now what presuppositions are implicit in this rhetorical treatment of metaphor? It is first admitted that words are to be taken in isolation from one another, each one having within itself a signification, which Aristotle calls its "current" meaning. By this he means that it is common to a certain population and fixed by the norms operative in that speaking community. Rhetoric begins, then, where the lexical code ends. It treats the figurative significations of a word, those significations which may subsequently become part of ordinary usage. The underlying question here is to account for these variations in significations. Why do these deviations from the ordinary, these figures of style, occur? The ancient rhetoricians generally replied that it was the purpose of a figure either to fill a semantic lacuna in the lexical code or to ornament discourse and make it more pleasing. Because we have more ideas than we have words to express them, we have to stretch the significations of those we do have beyond their ordinary use. Or, in those cases where a suitable word is already available, we might choose to use a figurative word in order to please or perhaps to seduce our audience. This second strategy of rhetorical figures reflects one of the central aspects of the general function of rhetoric, namely, persuasion. That is, rhetoric is a means of influencing an audience through the use of means of discourse which are not those of proof or violence. It aims at making the probable more attractive.

Metaphor is one of these rhetorical figures, the one where resemblance serves as the reason for substituting a figurative word for a missing or an absent literal word. It must be distinguished from the other figures of style, such as metonymy, for example, where contiguity takes the place that resemblance occupies in metaphor.

This is a very schematic summary of the long history of rhetoric, which begins with the Greek sophists and is continued by Aristotle, Cicero, and Quintilian, until it dies away in the nineteenth century. What remains constant in this tradition, however, can be schematized in the following six propositions.

(1) Metaphor is a trope, a figure of discourse that concerns denomination.

(2) It represents the extension of the meaning of a name through deviation from the literal meaning of words.

(3) The reason for this deviation is resemblance.

(4) The function of resemblance is to ground the substitution of the figurative meaning of a word in place of the literal meaning, which could have been used in the same place.

(5) Hence the substituted signification does not represent any semantic innovation. We can translate a metaphor, i.e., replace the literal meaning for which the figurative word is a substitute. In effect, substitution plus restitution equals zero.

(6) Since it does not represent a semantic innovation, a metaphor does not furnish any new information about reality. This is why it can be counted as one of the emotive functions of discourse.

These are the presuppositions of classical rhetoric which a modern semantic treatment of metaphor calls into question. This new semantics finds its best expression in the works of authors such as I.A. Richards, Max Black, Monroe Beardsley, Colin Turbayne, and Philip Wheelwright, among others.[4] And among these authors, it is the work of Richards that is truly pioneering because it marks the overthrow of the traditional problematic.

If Richards could reject the last two implications of the classical model — that a metaphor does not involve any new information and that therefore its function is purely decorative—it was because he broke away from the initial presuppositions.

The first presupposition to be rejected is that a metaphor is simply an accident of denomination, a displacement in the signification of words. With this presupposition classical rhetoric limited itself to the description of an effect of meaning that is really the result of the impact on the word of a production of meaning that takes place at the level of a complete utterance or sentence. This is the first discovery of a semantic approach to metaphor. Metaphor has to do with semantics of the sentence before it concerns the semantics of a word. And since a metaphor only makes sense in an utterance, it is a phenomenon of predication, not denomination. When the poet speaks of a "blue angelus," or a "mantle of sorrow," he puts two terms, which, following Richards, we may call the tenor and the vehicle, in tension. And only the ensemble constitutes the metaphor. So we should not really speak of the metaphorical use of a word, but rather of the metaphorical utterance. The metaphor is the result of the tension between two terms in a metaphorical utterance.

This first thesis implies a second. If a metaphor only concerns words because it is first produced at the level of a complete sentence, then the first phenomenon to consider is not any deviation from the literal meaning of the words, but the very functioning of the operation of predication at the level of the sentence. What we have just called the tension in a metaphorical utterance is really not something that occurs between two terms in the utterance, but rather between two opposed interpretations of the utterance. It is the conflict between these two interpretations that sustains the metaphor. In this regard, we can even say, in a general fashion, that the strategy of discourse by means of which the metaphoric utterance obtains its result is absurdity. This absurdity is only revealed through the attempt to interpret the utterance literally. The angelus is not blue, if blue is a color; sorrow is not a mantle, if the mantle is a garment made of cloth. Thus a metaphor does not exist in itself, but in and through an interpretation. The metaphorical interpretation presupposes a literal interpretation which self-destructs in a significant contradiction. It is this process of self-destruction or transformation which imposes a sort of twist on the words, an extension of meaning thanks to which we can make sense where a literal interpretation would be literally nonsensical. Hence a metaphor appears as a kind of riposte to a certain inconsistency in the metaphorical utterance literally interpreted. With Jean Cohen, we can call this inconsistency a "semantic impertinence," or to use a more supple and inclusive expression than that, "contradiction" or "absurdity", which are used by Max Black and Monroe Beardsley.[5]

To summarize this thesis: taking into account the lexical values of the words in a metaphorical utterance, we can only make sense, i.e., we can only save the whole utterance, by submitting the words in question to a kind of work of meaning—which, following Beardsley, we have called a metaphorical twist — thanks to which the utterance begins to make sense.

It is now possible to return to the third presupposition of the classical rhetorical conception of metaphor, the role of resemblance. This has often been misunderstood. Often it has been reduced to the role of images in poetic discourse, so that for many critics, especially the older ones, studying an author's metaphors meant discussing the nomenclature of the images used to illustrate his ideas. But if metaphor does not consist in clothing an idea in an image, if it consists instead in reducing the shock engendered by two incompatible ideas, then it is in the reduction of this gap or difference that resemblance plays a role. What is at stake in a metaphorical utterance, in other words, is the appearance of kinship where ordinary vision does not perceive any relationship. The functioning of a metaphor is here close to what Gilbert Ryle has called a "category mistake." It is, in effect, a calculated error, which brings together things that do not go together and by means of this apparent misundersanding it causes a new, hitherto unnoticed, relation of meaning to spring up between the terms that previous systems of classification had ignored or not allowed.

When Shakespeare speaks of time as a beggar,[6] he teaches us to see time as . . . , to see time like a beggar. Two previously distant classes are here suddenly brought together and the work of resemblance consists precisely in this bringing together of what once was distant. Aristotle, thus, was correct in this regard when he said that to be good at inventing metaphors was to have an eye for resemblances.

From this description of the work of resemblance in metaphorical utterances, another opposition to the purely rhetorical conception of metaphor follows. For classical rhetoric, one will recall, a trope was the simple substitution of one word for another. But substitution is a sterile operation, whereas in a live metaphor the tension between the words, or, more precisely, between the two interpretations, one literal and the other metaphoric, at the level of the entire sentence, elicits a veritable creation of meaning of which classical rhetoric can only note the result. It cannot account for this creation of meaning. Within a tension theory of metaphor, however, such as we are here opposing to a substitution theory, a new signification emerges, which embraces the whole sentence. In this sense, a metaphor is an instantaneous creation, a semantic innovation which has no status in already established language and which only exists because of the attribution of an unusual or an unexpected predicate. Metaphor therefore is more like the resolution of an enigma than a simple association based on resemblance; it is constituted by the resolution of a semantic dissonance. We will not recognize the specificity of this phenomenon so long as we limit our consideration to dead metaphors, which are really no longer metaphors properly speaking. By a dead metaphor, I mean such expressions as "the foot of a chair" or "a mountain." Live metaphors are metaphors of invention within which the response to the discordance in the sentence is a new extension of meaning, although it is certainly true that such inventive metaphors tend to become dead metaphors through repetition. In such cases, the extended meaning becomes part of our lexicon and contributes to the polysemy of the words in question whose everyday meanings are thereby augmented. There are no live metaphors in a dictionary.

Two final conclusions may be drawn from this analysis, and they stand in opposition to the last two presuppositions of the classical theory. First, real metaphors are not translatable. Only metaphors of substitution are susceptible of a translation which could restore the literal signification. Tension metaphors are not translatable because they create their meaning. This is not to say that they cannot be paraphrased, just that such a paraphrase is infinite and incapable of exhausting the innovative meaning.

The second conclusion is that a metaphor is not an ornament of discourse. It has more than an emotive value because it offers new information. A metaphor, in short, tells us something new about reality.

From Metaphor to Symbol

The advantage of taking up the problem of double-meaning in terms of metaphors rather than symbols is twofold. First, metaphor has been the object of long and detailed study by rhetoricians; second, the renewal of this investigation by semantics, which takes up the structural problems left unresolved by rhetoric, is limited to those linguistic factors that give a homogeneous linguistic constitution to the phenomenon in question.

Such is not the case with symbols. The study of symbols runs into two difficulties which make any direct access to their double-meaning structure difficult. First, symbols belong to too many and too diverse fields of research. I considered three such fields in my earlier writings. Psychoanalysis, for instance, deals with dreams, other symptoms, and cultural objects akin to them as being symbolic of deep psychic conflicts. Poetics, on the other hand, if we understand this term in a broad sense, understands symbols to be the privileged images of a poem, or those images that dominate an author's works, or a school of literature, or the persistent figures within which a whole culture recognizes itself, or even the great archetypal images which humanity as a whole—ignoring cultural differences — celebrates.

At this point we are close to the third use of the word "symbol" by the history of religions. Mircea Eliade, for example, recognizes such concrete entities as trees, labyrinths, ladders, and mountains as symbols insofar as they represent symbols of space and time, or flight and transcendence, and point beyond themselves to something wholly other, which manifests itself in them. Thus the problem of symbols is dispersed among many fields of research and so divided among them that it tends to become lost in their proliferation.

The second difficulty with symbols is that the concept "symbol" brings together two dimensions, we might even say, two universes, of discourse, one linguistic and the other of a non-linguistic order. The linguistic character of symbols is attested to by the fact that it is indeed possible to construct a semantics of symbols, i.e., a theory that would account for their structure in terms of meaning or signification. Thus we can speak of the symbol as having a double meaning or a first and a second order meaning. But the non-linguistic dimension is just as obvious as the linguistic one. As the examples just cited indicate, a symbol always refers its linguistic element to something else. Thus psychoanalysis links its symbols to hidden psychic conflicts; while the literary critic refers to something like a vision of the world or a desire to transform all language into literature; and the historian of religion sees in symbols the milieu of manifestations of the Sacred, or what Eliade calls hierophanies.

It is just this external complexity of symbols which accounts for my effort to clarify them in light of the theory of metaphor.

This may be done in three steps. It is first possible to identify the semantic kernel characteristic of every symbol, however different each might be, on the basis of the structure of meaning operative in metaphorical utterances. Second, the metaphorical functioning of language will allow us to isolate the non-linguistic stratum of symbols, the principle of its dissemination, through a method of contrast. Finally, in return, this new understanding of symbols will give rise to further developments in the theory of metaphor, which would otherwise remain concealed. In this way the theory of symbols will allow us to complete that of metaphor.

I hypothesize that these developments will provide enough of the missing intermediary steps to allow us to bridge the gap between metaphors and symbols.

The Semantic Moment of a Symbol

The relation between the literal meaning and the figurative meaning of a metaphorical utterance provides an appropriate guideline which will allow us to identify the properly semantic traits of a symbol. These traits are the ones that relate every form of symbol to a language, thereby assuring the unity of symbols despite their being dispersed among the numerous places where they emerge or appear. The appearance of this semantic dimension is the result of a theoretical approach so long as we still confuse the semantic nature of symbols with their other traits which resist any transposition to language. The symbol, in effect, only gives rise to thought if it first gives rise to speech. Metaphor is the appropriate re-agent to bring to light this aspect of symbols that has an affinity for language.

Here a tension theory of metaphor is more useful than a substitution theory. The metaphorical twist, which our words must undergo in response to the semantic impertinence at the level of the entire sentence, can be taken as the model for the extension of meaning operative in every symbol. In the three areas of investigation cited above, for example, a symbol, in the most general sense, functions as a "surplus of significa-tion." Freud's treatment of little Hans' wolf signifies more than we mean when we describe a wolf. The sea in ancient Babylonian myths signifies more than the expanse of water that can be seen from the shore. And a sunrise in a poem by Wordsworth signifies more than a simple meteorological phenomenon.

As in metaphor theory, this excess of signification in a symbol can be opposed to the literal signification, but only on the condition that we also oppose two interpretations at the same time. Only for an interpretation are there two levels of signification since it is the recognition of the literal meaning that allows us to see that a symbol still contains more mean-ing. This surplus of meaning is the residue of the literal interpretation. Yet for the one who participates in the sym-bolic signification there are really not two significations, one literal and the other symbolic, but rather a single movement, which transfers him from one level to the other and which assimilates him to the second signification by means of, or through, the literal one.

Symbolic signification, therefore, is so constituted that we can only attain the secondary signification by way of the primary signification, where this primary signification is the sole means of access to the surplus of meaning. The primary signification gives the secondary signification, in effect, as the meaning of a meaning. This trait marks the difference between a symbol and an allegory. Allegory is a rhetorical procedure that can be eliminated once it has done its job. Having ascended the ladder, we can then descend it. Allegory is a didactic procedure. It facilitates learning, but can be ignored in any directly conceptual approach. In contrast, there is no symbolic knowledge except when it is impossible to directly grasp the concept and when the direction towards the concept is indirectly indicated by the secondary signification of a primary signification.

Next, the work of resemblance characteristic of symbols can also be associated with the corresponding process in metaphors. The interplay of similarity and dissimilarity presents, in effect, the conflict between some prior categorization of reality and a new one just being born. As one author has put it, metaphor is an idyll with a new partner who resists while giving in. And metaphor has long been compared to stereoscopic vision where the different concepts may be said to come together to give the appearance of solidity and depth.

In a symbol, it is true that these relations are more confused, not being as nicely articulated on a logical level. This is why we speak of assimilation rather than apprehension: the symbol assimilates rather than apprehends a resemblance. Moreover, in assimilating some things to others it assimilates us to what is thereby signified. This is precisely what makes the theory of symbols so fascinating, yet deceiving. All the boundaries are blurred — between the things as well as between the things and ourselves. Later we will be able to catch hold of one of the factors operative here when we turn to the non-linguistic stratum of symbols.

If the theory of metaphor is as clarifying as I say it is, it is because a work of language has already taken place, a work which places things at a distance from the utterance and which, within the utterance, distanciates the predicate from the subject. In fact, to speak of metaphor as a bizarre form of predication is already to invoke some principle of articulation which is lacking in the symbolic order.

Once again it is the metaphorical functioning of language that allows us to justice to another trait of symbols, which is obstinately emphasized by their defenders, yet for which they lack the key. We readily concede that a symbol cannot be exhaustively treated by conceptual language, that there is more in a symbol than in any of its conceptual equivalents; a trait which is eagerly embraced by the opponents of conceptual thinking. For them, one must choose: either the symbol or the concept. But metaphor theory leads us to a different conclusion. It shows how new possibilities for articulating and conceptualizing reality can arise through an assimilation of hitherto separated semantic fields. Far from being a part of conceptual thinking, such semantic innovation marks the emergence of such thought. This is why the theory of symbols is led into the neighborhood of the Kantian theory of the schematism and conceptual synthesis by the theory of metaphor. There is no need to deny the concept in order to admit that symbols give rise to an endless exegesis. If no concept can exhaust the requirement of further thinking borne by symbols, this idea signifies only that no given categorization can embrace all the semantic possibilities of a symbol. But it is the work of the concept alone that can testify to this surplus of meaning.

The Non-Semantic Moment of a Symbol

It now is possible to identify the non-semantic side of symbols, if we continue our method of contrasts, and if we agree to call semantic those traits of symbols which (1) lend themselves to linguistic and logical analysis in terms of signification and interpretation, and (2) overlap the corresponding traits of metaphors. For something in a symbol does not correspond to a metaphor and, because of this fact, resists any linguistic, semantic, or logical transcription.

This opacity of a symbol is related to the rootedness of symbols in areas of our experience that are open to different methods of investigation. That psychoanalysis should consider dreams as the paradigm for substituted and disguised representations, for example, presupposes that one first takes sleep into consideration as the context for oneiric activity. Poetic images are no less bound to a global form of behavior which in German is called *dichten* (to compose or write poetry; literally "to poeticize"). And would we have religious sym-

57

bols if man had not given himself over to very complex, yet specific forms of behavior designed to invoke, implore, or repulse the supernatural forces, which dwell in the depths of human existence, transcending and dominating it?

Thus in a variety of ways symbolic activity lacks autonomy. It is a bound activity, and it is the task of many disciplines to reveal the lines that attach the symbolic function to this or that non-symbolic or pre-linguistic activity.

The case of psychoanalysis is especially illuminating, although I will not dwell at length upon it here since I have dealt with it in detail elsewhere. I will only say that in psycho-analysis symbolic activity is a boundary phenomenon linked to the boundary between desire and culture, which is itself a boundary between impulses and their delegated or affective representatives. This is the boundary between primary re-pression — which affects the first witnesses of our impulses — and secondary repression, which is repression properly speaking — that repression which occurs after the fact and which only allows derivative offshoots, indefinite substitute signs, or signs of signs to appear. This position of the psychoanalytic sign on the boundary between a conflict of impulses and an interplay of signifiers means that psycho-analysis must develop a mixed language, which connects the vocabulary of the dynamics or energetics — we might even speak of a hydraulics — of impulses with that of a textural exegesis. And many psychoanalytical terms bear the mark of this double origin. *The Interpretation of Dreams*, for instance, introduces the concept of censorship, which expresses the repressive action of a force at the level of the production of a text, albeit a text which is first revealed as erased or disfig-ured.

Similarly, we might point to those diverse procedures Freud placed under the generic title of the "dream work." As work, these procedures operate mechanically as displacements, condensation, decomposition, etc., procedures that Freud sums up under the general heading *Entstellung*, which has been translated as "distortion" or "deformation". At the same time, however, this interplay of forces can be read in the text of the dream account understood as a kind of palimpsest, riddle, or hieroglyph. Psychoanalysis must, therefore, assume the mixed epistemological status which these hybrid concepts impose upon it insofar as these deep conflicts resist any reduction to linguistic processes, yet cannot be read anywhere else than in the dream or symbolic text. Such a mixed conceptualization does not betray some fault in the conceptualization of psychoanalysis, but on the contrary the exact recognition of the place where its discourse occurs: in the intermingling of force and meaning, impulse and discourse, energetics and semantics.

This brief discussion of psychoanalysis allows us to grasp one reason why the symbol does not pass over into metaphor. Metaphor occurs in the already purified universe of the *logos*, while the symbol hesistates on the dividing line between *bios* and *logos*. It testifies to the primordial rootedness of Discourse in Life. It is born where force and form coincide.

It is more difficult to say what makes poetic language a "bound" language. As a first approximation, in fact, it is an unbound or liberated language that is freed from certain lexical, syntactical, and stylistic constraints. It is freed, above all, from the intended references of both ordinary and scientific language, which, we may say by way of contrast, are bound by the facts, empirical objects, and logical constraints of our established ways of thinking. But may we also not say, again by way of contrast, that the poetic world is just as hypothetical a space as is the mathematical order in relation to any given world? The poet, in short, operates through language in a hypothetical realm. In an extreme form we might even say that the poetic project is one of destroying the world as we ordinarily take it for granted, just as Husserl made the destruction of our world the basis of the phenomenological reduction. Or without going quite so far, we could say, following Northrop Frye, that as the inversion of ordinary language, poetic language is not directed outwards, but inwards towards an interior, which is nothing other than the mood structured and expressed by a poem. Here a poem is like a work of music in that its mood is exactly coextensive with the internal order of symbols articulated by its language.

It is in this sense that poetry is liberated from the world. But if it is liberated in this sense, in another sense it is bound, and it is bound precisely to the extent that it is also liberated. What has just been said about the mood, which is coextensive with the symbolic order of a poem, shows that a poem is not some gratuitous form of verbal word play. Rather, the poem is bound by what it creates, if the suspension of ordinary discourse and its didactic intention assumes an urgent character for the poet, this is just because the reduction of the referential values of ordinary discourse is the negative condition that allows new configurations expressing the meaning of reality to be brought to language. Through those new configurations new ways of being in the world, of living there, and of projecting our innermost possibilities onto it are also brought to language. Therefore to limit ourselves to saying that a poem structures and expresses a mood is not to say much, for what is a mood if it is not a specific manner of being in the world and relating oneself to it, of understanding it and interpreting it? What binds poetic discourse, then, is the need to bring to language modes of being that ordinary vision obscures or even represses. And in this sense, no one is more free than the poet. We might even say that the poet's speech is freed from the ordinary vision of the world only because he makes himself free for the new being which he has to bring to language.

Finally, the symbolism of the Sacred as it has been studied, for example, by Mircea Eliade is particularly appropriate for our meditation on the rootedness of discourse in a nonsemantic order. Even before Eliade, Rudolf Otto, in his book, *The Idea of the Holy*, strongly emphasized the appearance of the Sacred as power, strength, efficacity. Whatever objections we might raise about his description of the Sacred, it is valuable in that it helps us to be on guard against all attempts to reduce mythology linguistically. We are warned from the very beginning that we are here crossing the threshold of an experience that does not allow itself to be completely inscribed within the categories of *logos* or proclamation and its transmission or interpretation. The numinous element is not first a question of language, if it ever really becomes one, for to speak of power is to speak of something other than speech even if it implies the power of speaking. This power as efficacity *par excellence* is what does not pass over completely into the articulation of meaning.

It is true that the notion of hierophany, which Eliade substitutes for the too massive notion of the numinous, does imply that manifestations of the Sacred have a form or structure, but even then no special privilege is bestowed upon speech. The Sacred may equally well manifest itself in stones or trees as bearers of efficacity.

The preverbal character of such an experience is attested to by the very modulations of space and time as sacred space and sacred time, which result and which are inscribed beneath language at the aesthetic level of experience, in the Kantian sense of this expression.

The bond between myth and ritual attests in another way to this non-linguistic dimension of the Sacred. It functions as a logic of correspondences, which characterize the sacred universe and indicate the specificity of *homo religiosus's* vision of the world. Such ties occur at the level of the very elements of the natural world such as the sky, earth, air, and water. And the same uranian symbolism makes the diverse epiphanies communicate among themselves, while at the same time they also refer to the divine immanent in the hierophanies of life. Thus to divine transcendence there is opposed a proximate sacred as attested to by the fertility of the soil, vegetative exuberance, the flourishing of the flocks, and the fecundity of the maternal womb.

Within the sacred universe there are not living creatures here and there, but life is everywhere as a sacrality, which permeates everything and which is seen in the movement of the stars, the return to life of vegetation each year, and the alternation of birth and death. It is in this sense that symbols are bound within the sacred universe: the symbols only come to language to the extent that the elements of the world themselves become transparent.

This bound character of symbols makes all the difference between a symbol and a metaphor. The latter is a free invention of discourse; the former is bound to the cosmos. Here we touch an irreducible element, an element more irreducible than the one that poetic experience uncovers. In the sacred universe the capacity to speak is founded upon the capacity of the cosmos to signify. The logic of meaning, therefore, follows from the very structure of the sacred universe. Its law is the law of correspondences, correspondences between creation *in illo tempore* and the present order of natural appearances and human activities. This is why, for example, a temple always conforms to some celestial model. And why the hierogamy of earth and sky corresponds to the union between male and female as a correspondence between the macrocosm and the microcosm. Similarly there is a correspondence between the tillable soil and the feminine organ, between the fecundity of the earth and the maternal womb, between the sun and our eyes, semen and seeds, burial and the sowing of grain, birth and the return of spring.

There is a triple correspondence between the body, houses, and the cosmos, which makes the pillars of a temple and our spinal columns symbolic of one another, just as there are correspondences between a roof and the skull, breath and wind, etc. This triple correspondence is also the reason why thresholds, doors, bridges, and narrow pathways outlined by the very act of inhabiting space and dwelling in it correspond to the homologous kinds of passage which rites of initiation help us to cross over in the critical moments of our pilgrimage through life: moments such as birth, puberty, marriage, and death.

Such is the logic of correspondences, which binds discourse in the universe of the Sacred. We might even say that it is always by means of discourse that this logic manifests itself for if no myth narrated how things came to be or if there were no rituals which re-enacted this process, the Sacred would remain unmanifested. As regards ritual, which as such is one modality of making or doing—a doing of something marked by power, it would lack the power to organize space and time without an instituting word, without a discourse which tells how one should act in response to the manifestation of power. And as regards the symbolism that circulates among the elements of the world, this too brings into play a whole work of language. Even more, symbolism only works when its structure is interpreted. In this sense a minimal hermeneutic is required for the functioning of any symbolism. But this linguistic articulation does not suppress what I have called the adherence to symbolism characteristic of the sacred universe, rather it presupposes it. Interpretation of a symbolism cannot even get under way if its work of mediation were not legitimated by an immediate liaison between the appearance and the meaning in the hierophany under consideration. The sacredness of nature reveals itself in saying itself symbolically. The revealing grounds the saying, not the reverse.

If we now bring together the preceding analyses, I am inclined to say that what asks to be brought to language in symbols, but which never passes over completely into language, is always something powerful, efficacious, forceful. Man, it seems, is here designated as a power to exist, indirectly discerned from above, below, and laterally. The power of impulses which haunt our phantasies, of imaginary modes of being which ignite the poetic word, and of the all-embracing, that most powerful something which menaces us so long as we feel unloved, in all these registers and perhaps in others as well, the dialectic of power and form takes place, which insures that language only captures the foam on the surface of life.

The Intermediate Degrees between Symbol and Metaphor

My last remarks — as adventured and adventurous as they might be — render the whole enterprise of elucidating symbols in light of the theory of metaphor vain if the description of symbols does not solicit in return some new developments in metaphor theory.

This feedback of the theory of symbols on the theory of metaphor first invites us to reflect upon the functioning of metaphors in a chain or network. In the analysis proposed above, metaphors remain dispersed events, in a way, places in discourse. The comparison of metaphor to an enigma or a riddle tends to limit the analysis to individual windfalls, and therefore to a transitory aspect of language. In fact, by calling metaphor a semantic innovation, we emphasize the fact that it only exists in the moment of invention. Lacking any status in established language, a metaphor is in the strong sense of the word, an event of discourse. The result is that when a metaphor is taken up and accepted by a linguistic community it tends to become confused with an extension of the polysemy of words. It first becomes a trivial, then a dead metaphor. Symbols, in contrast, because they plunge their roots into the durable constellations of life, feeling, and the universe, and because they have such an incredible stability, lead us to think that a symbol never dies, it is only transformed. Hence if we were to hold fast to our criteria for a metaphor, symbols must be dead metaphors. If not, what makes the difference?

Metaphorical functioning would be completely inadequate as a way of expressing the different temporality of symbols, what we might call their insistence, if metaphors did not save themselves from complete evanescence by means of a whole array of intersignifications. One metaphor, in effect, calls for another and each one stays alive by conserving its power to evoke the whole network. Thus within the Hebraic tradition God is called King, Father, Husband, Lord, Shepherd, and Judge as well as Rock, Fortress, Redeemer, and Suffering Servant. The network engenders what we can call root metaphors, metaphors which, on the one hand, have the power to bring together the partial metaphors borrowed from the diverse fields of our experience and thereby to assure them a kind of equilibrium. On the other hand, they have the ability to engender a conceptual diversity, I mean, an unlimited number of potential interpretations at a conceptual level. Root metaphors assemble and scatter. They assemble subordinate images together, and they scatter concepts at a higher level. They are the dominant metaphors capable of both engendering and organizing a network that serves as a junction between the symbolic level with its slow evolution and the more volatile metaphorical level.

There is a second aspect of metaphorical functioning that also tends to bring it closer to symbols. Beyond its constituting a network, a set of metaphors presents an original hierarchical constitution, as Philip Wheelwright has strongly emphasized in his works on metaphor, *The Burning Fountain*, and, especially, *Metaphor and Reality*.[8] It is possible to describe the metaphoric game at various levels of organization depending upon whether we consider the metaphors in isolated sentences, or as underlying a given poem, or as the dominant metaphors of a poet, or the typical metaphors of a particular linguistic community or a given culture, which can extend so far as to include large cultural spheres such as Christianity. Finally, certain metaphors are so radical that they seem to haunt all human discourse. These metaphors, which Wheelwright calls archetypes, become indistinguishable from the symbolic paradigms Eliade studies in his *Patterns in Comparative Religion*.[9]

So it appears as though certain fundamental human experiences make up an immediate symbolism that presides over the most primitive metaphorical order. This originary symbolism seems to adhere to the most immutable human manner of being in the world, whether it be a question of above and below, the cardinal directions, the spectacle of the heavens, terrestrial localization, houses, paths, fire, wind, stones, or water. If we add that this anthropological and cosmic symbolism is in a kind of subterranean communication with our libidinal sphere and through it with what Freud called the combat between the giants, the gigantomachy between eros and death, we will see why the metaphorical order is submitted to what we can call a request for work by this symbolic experience. Everything indicates that symbolic experience calls for a work of meaning from metaphor, a work which it partially provides through its organizational network and its hierarchical levels. Everything indicates that symbol systems constitute a reservoir of meaning whose metaphoric potential is yet to be spoken. And, in fact, the history of words and culture would seem to indicate that if language never constitutes the most superficial layer of our symbolic experience, this deep layer only becomes accessible to us to the extent that it is formed and articulated at a linguistic and literary level since the most insistent metaphors hold fast to the intertwining of the symbolic infrastructure and metaphoric superstructure.

65

The theory of metaphor can finally be extended in a third way in the direction of the most specific traits of symbols. Numerous authors have remarked upon the kinship between metaphors and models. This kinship plays a decisive role, for example, in the work of Max Black, which is even entitled *Models and Metaphors*.[10] And from his side, the English theologian Ian Ramsey has attempted to elucidate the function of religious language by revising Max Black's theory in an appropriate fashion.[11]

Such a rapprochement between models and metaphors allows us to develop the theory of metaphor in a direction hitherto neglected in our brief presentation of this theory, I mean its referential dimension. If we adopt the distinction introduced by Frege between sense and reference—the sense being the pure predicative relation, the reference its pretention to say something about reality, in short, its truth value—it appears as if every discourse can be investigated in terms of both its internal organization, which makes it a message, which can be identified and reidentified, and its referential intention, which is its pretention to say something about something.[12]

Now Max Black says that a model has the same structure of sense as a metaphor, but it constitutes the referential dimension of a metaphor. What is this referential value? It is a part of the heuristic function, that is, the aspect of discovery, of a metaphor and a model, of a metaphor as a model.

In scientific language, a model is essentially a heuristic procedure that serves to overthrow an inadequate interpretation and to open the way to a new and more adequate one. In Mary Hesse's terms, it is an instrument of redescription, an expression that I will use in the remainder of this analysis.[13] But it is important to understand that this term is to be taken in its strictly epistemological use.

The redescriptive power of a model can only be understood if, following Max Black, we carefully distinguish between three sorts of models: scale models, as, for example, a model boat; analogical models, which deal with structural identity, as, for example, a schematic diagram in electronics; and finally, theoretical models, which from an epistemological point of view, are the real models and which consist of construing an imaginary object more accessible to description as a more complex domain of reality whose properties correspond to the properties of the object. As Max Black puts it, to describe a domain of reality in terms of an imaginary theoretical model is a way of seeing things differently by changing our language about the subject of our investigation. This change of language proceeds from the construction of a heuristic fiction and through the transposition of the characteristics of this heuristic fiction to reality itself.

Let us apply this concept of model to metaphor. The guideline here is the relation between the two notions of a heuristic fiction and the redescription that occurs through the transference of this fiction to reality. It is this double movement that we also find in metaphor, for "a memorable metaphor has the power to bring two separate domains into cognitive and emotional relation by using language directly appropriate for the one as a lens for seeing the other. . . ."[14] Thanks to this detour through the heuristic fiction we perceive new connections among things. The basis of this transfer is the presumed isomorphism between the model and its domain of application. It is this isomorphism that legitimates the "analogical transfer of a vocabulary" and that allows a metaphor to function like a model and "reveal new relationships."[15]

Let us carry this analysis even further in its application to metaphor. Considered in terms of its referential bearing, poetic language has in common with scientific language that it only reaches reality through a detour that serves to deny our ordinary vision and the language we normally use to describe it. In doing this both poetic and scientific language aim at a reality more real than appearances. The theory of models thus allows us to satisfactorily interpret the paradox of poetic language evoked earlier. This paradox, we said, following Northrop Frye and other literary critics, gives poetic discourse a centripetal direction opposed to the centrifugal direction, which characterizes descriptive and didactic discourse. This is why poetry creates its own world. The suspension of the referential function of the first degree affects ordinary language to the benefit of a second degree reference, which is attached precisely to the fictive dimension revealed by the theory of models. In the same way that the literal sense has to be left behind so that the metaphorical sense can emerge, so the literal reference must collapse so that the heuristic fiction can work its redescription of reality.

In the case of metaphor, this redescription is guided by the interplay between differences and resemblances that gives rise to the tension at the level of the utterance. It is precisely from this tensive apprehension that a new vision of reality springs forth, which ordinary vision resists because it is attached to the ordinary use of words. The eclipse of the objective, manipulable world thus makes way for the revelation of a new dimension of reality and truth.

In speaking this way I am saying nothing more than Aristotle said when dealing with tragedy in his *Poetics*. The composition of a story or a plot—Aristotle speaks here of a *mythos*—is the shortest path to mimesis, which is the central ideal of all poetry. In other words, poetry only imitates reality by recreating it on a mythical level of discourse. Here fiction and redescription go hand in hand.

Must we not conclude then that metaphor implies a tensive use of language in order to uphold a tensive concept of reality? By this I mean that the tension is not simply between words, but within the very copula of the metaphorical utterance. "Nature is a temple where living pillars . . ." Here "is" signifies both is and is not. The literal "is" is overturned by the absurdity and surmounted by a metaphorical "is" equivalent to "is like . . ." Thus poetic language does not tell how things literally are, but what they are like. Can we not then call insistent metaphors—those metaphors that are closest to the symbolic depths of our existence—metaphors that owe their privilege of revealing what things are like to their organization into networks and hierarchical levels?

To conclude, I will say that we must accept two contrary propositions concerning the relationship between metaphors and symbols. On one side, there is more in the metaphor than in the symbol; on the other side, there is more in the symbol than in the metaphor.

There is more in the metaphor than in the symbol in the sense that it brings to language the implicit semantics of the symbol. What remains confused in the symbol—the assimilation of one thing to another, and of us to things; the endless correspondence between the elements — is clarified in the tension of the metaphorical utterance.

But there is more in the symbol than in the metaphor. Metaphor is just the linguistic procedure—that bizarre form of predication — within which the symbolic power is deposited. The symbol remains a two-dimensional phenomenon to the extent that the semantic face refers back to the non-semantic one. The symbol is bound in a way that the metaphor is not. Symbols have roots. Symbols plunge us into the shadowy experience of power. Metaphors are just the linguistic surface of symbols, and they owe their power to relate the semantic surface to the presemantic surface in the depths of human experience to the two-dimensional structure of the symbol.

4.

EXPLANATION AND UNDERSTANDING

The final problem to be dealt with in this series of essays concerns the range of attitudes that a reader may entertain when confronted with a text. In the previous essays the emphasis was on the speaker, writer, or author and the questions dealt with were: What is meant when somebody speaks? When somebody writes? When somebody means more than what he actually says? Now we ask what is it to understand a discourse when that discourse is a text or a literary work? How do we make sense of written discourse?

Beyond Romanticist Hermeneutics

With the dialectic of explanation and understanding, I hope to provide my interpretation theory with an analysis of writing, which will be the counterpart of that of the text as a work of discourse. To the extent that the act of reading is the counterpart of the act of writing, the dialectic of event and meaning, so essential to the structure of discourse, as we saw in the first essay, generates a correlative dialectic in reading between understanding or comprehension (the *verstehen* of the German hermeneutical tradition) and explanation (the *erklären* of that same tradition). Without imposing too mechanical a correspondence between the inner structure of the text as the discourse of the writer and the process of interpretation as the discourse of the reader on our discussion, it may be said, at least in an introductory fashion, that understanding is to reading what the event of discourse is to the utterance of discourse and that explanation is to reading what the verbal and textual autonomy is to the objective meaning of discourse. A dialectical structure of reading therefore corresponds to the dialectical structure of discourse. This correspondence confirms my statement in my prefatory remarks that the theory of discourse presented in the first essay governs all the subsequent developments of my interpetation theory.

Just as the dialectic of event and meaning remains implicit and difficult to recognize in oral discourse, that of explanation and understanding is quite impossible to identify in the dialogical situation that we call conversation. We explain something to someone else in order that he can understand. And what he has understood, he can in turn explain to a third party. Thus understanding and explanation tend to overlap and to pass over into each other. I will surmise, however, that in explanation we ex-plicate or unfold the range of propositions and meanings, whereas in understanding we comprehend or grasp as a whole the chain of partial meanings in one act of synthesis.

This nascent, inchoative polarity between explanation and understanding as it is dimly perceived in the communication process of conversation becomes a clearly contrasting duality in Romanticist hermeneutics. Each term of the pair there represents a distinct and irreducible mode of intelligibility.

Explanation finds its paradigmatic field of application in the natural sciences. When there are external facts to observe, hypotheses to be submitted to empirical verification, general laws for covering such facts, theories to encompass the scattered laws in a systematic whole, and subordination of empirical generalizations to hypothetic-deductive procedures, then we may say that we "explain." And the appropriate correlate of explanation is nature understood as the common horizon of facts, laws and theories, hypotheses, verifications, and deductions.

Understanding, in contrast, finds its originary field of application in the human sciences (the German *Geisteswissenschaften*), where science has to do with the experience of other subjects or other minds similar to our own. It relies on the meaningfulness of such forms of expression as physiognomic, gestural, vocal, or written signs, and upon documents and monuments, which share with writing the general character of inscription. The immediate types of expression are meaningful because they refer directly to the experience of the other mind which they convey. The other, less direct sources such as written signs, documents, and monuments are no less significant, except that they convey the other mind's experiences indirectly, not directly, to us. The necessity of interpreting these signs proceeds precisely from the indirectness of the way in which they convey such experiences. But there would be no problem of interpretation, taken as a derivative of understanding, if the indirect sources were not indirect expressions of a psychic life, homogenous to the immediate expressions of a foreign psychic life. This continuity between direct and indirect signs explains why "empathy" as the transference of ourselves into another's psychic life is the principle common to every kind of understanding, whether direct or indirect.

The dichotomy between understanding and explanation in Romanticist hermeneutics is both epistemological and ontological. It opposes two methodologies and two spheres of reality, nature and mind. Interpretation is not a third term, nor, as I shall attempt to demonstrate, the name of the dialectic between explanation and understanding. Interpretation is a particular case of understanding. It is understanding applied to the written expressions of life. In a theory of signs that de-emphasizes the difference between speaking and writing, and above all that does not stress the dialectic of event and meaning, it can be expected that interpretation only appears as one province within the empire of comprehension or understanding.

A different distribution of the concepts of understanding, explanation, and interpretation is suggested, however, by the maxim derived from my analysis in the first essay that if discourse is produced as an event, it is understood as meaning. Here mutual understanding relies on sharing in the same sphere of meaning. Already in oral conversation, for example, the transfer into a foreign psychic life finds support in the sameness of the shared sphere of meaning. The dialectic of explanation and understanding has already begun. To understand the utterer's meaning and to understand the utterance meaning constitute a circular process. The development of explanation as an autonomous process proceeds from the exteriorization of the event in the meaning, which is made complete by writing and the generative codes of literature. Then understanding, which is more directed towards the intentional unity of discourse, and explanation, which is more directed towards the analytic structure of the text, tend to become the distinct poles of a developed dichotomy. But this dichotomy does not go so far as to destroy the initial dialectic of the utter's and the utterance meaning. As we saw in the second and third essays, this dialectic is mediated by more and more intermediary terms, but never canceled. In the same way the polarity between explanation and understanding in reading must not be treated in dualistic terms, but as a complex and highly mediated dialectic. Then the term interpretation may be applied, not to a particular case of understanding, that of the written expressions of life, but to the whole process that encompasses explanation and understanding. Interpretation as the dialectic of explanation and understanding or comprehension may then be traced back to the initial stages of interpretative behavior already at work in conversation. And while it is true that only writing and literary composition provide a full development of this dialectic, interpretation must not be referred to as a province of understanding. It is not defined by a kind of object — "inscribed" signs in the most general sense of the term — but by a kind of process: the dynamic of interpretative reading.

For the sake of a didactic exposition of the dialectic of explanation and understanding, as phases of a unique process, I propose to describe this dialectic first as a move from understanding to explaining and then as a move from explanation to comprehension. The first time, understanding will be a naive grasping of the meaning of the text as a whole. The second time, comprehension will be a sophisticated mode of understanding, supported by explanatory procedures. In the beginning, understanding is a guess. At the end, it satisfies the concept of appropriation, which was described in the

74

third essay as the rejoinder to the kind of distanciation linked to the full objectification of the text. Explanation, then, will appear as the mediation between two stages of understanding. If isolated from this concrete process, it is a mere abstraction, an artifact of methodology.

From Guess to Validation

Why must the first act of understanding take the form of a guess? And what has to be guessed in a text?

The necessity of guessing the meaning of a text may be related to the kind of semantic autonomy that I ascribed to the textual meaning in my second essay. With writing, the verbal meaning of the text no longer coincides with the mental meaning or intention of the text. This intention is both fulfilled and abolished by the text, which is no longer the voice of someone present. The text is mute. An asymmetric relation obtains between text and reader, in which only one of the partners speaks for the two. The text is like a musical score and the reader like the orchestra conductor who obeys the instructions of the notation. Consequently, to understand is not merely to repeat the speech event in a similar event, it is to generate a new event beginning from the text in which the intial event has been objectified.

In other words, we have to guess the meaning of the text because the author's intention is beyond our reach. Here perhaps my opposition to Romanticist hermeneutics is most forceful. We all know the maxim—which indeed antedates the Romantics, since Kant knows and cites it[1]—to understand an author better than he understood himself. Now even if this maxim may receive different interpretations, even if it may be retained with proper qualifications (as I shall attempt to show below), it led hermeneutics astray inasmuch as it expressed the ideal of "congeniality" or a communion from "genius" to "genius" in interpretation. The Romanticist forms of hermeneutics overlooked the specific situation created by the disjunction of the verbal meaning of the text from the mental intention of the author. The fact is that the author can no longer "rescue" his work, to recall Plato's image, which I

75

discussed in the second essay. His intention is often unknown to us, sometimes redundant, sometimes useless, and sometimes even harmful as regards the interpretation of the verbal meaning of his work. In even the better cases it has to be taken into account in light of the text itself.

In conclusion, then, there is a problem of interpretation not so much because of the incommunicability of the psychic experience of the author, but because of the very nature of the verbal intention of the text. The surpassing of the intention by the meaning signifies precisely that understanding takes place in a nonpsychological and properly semantical space, which the text has carved out by severing itself from the mental intention of its author.

The dialectic of *erklären* and *verstehen* begins here. If the objective meaning is something other than the subjective intention of the author, it may be construed in various ways. Misunderstanding is possible and even unavoidable. The problem of the correct understanding can no longer be solved by a simple return to the alleged situation of the author. The concept of guess has no other origin. To construe the meaning as the verbal meaning of the text is to make a guess.

But, as well shall see below, if there are no rules for making good guesses, there are methods for validating those guesses we do make.[2] In this new dialectic both terms are required. Guessing corresponds to what Schleiermacher called the "divinatory," validation to what he called the "grammatical." Both are necessary to the process of reading a text.

The transition from guessing to explaining is secured by an investigation of the specific object of guessing. We have answered our first question, why do we have to guess in order to understand? We still have to say what is to be guessed by understanding.

First, to construe the verbal meaning of a text is to construe it as a whole. Here we rely more on the analysis of discourse as work than on the analysis of discourse as written. A work of discourse is more than a linear sequence of sentences. It is a cumulative, holistic process.

Since this specific structure of the work cannot be derived from that of the single sentences, the text as such has a kind of plurivocity, which is other than the polysemy of individual words, and other than the ambiguity of individual sentences. This textual plurivocity is typical of complex works of discourse and opens them to a plurality of constructions. The relation between whole and parts — as in a work of art or an animal — requires a specific kind of "judgment" for which Kant has given the theory in the *Critique of Judgment*. Concretely, the whole appears as a hierarchy of topics, of primary and subordinate topics that are not, so to speak, at the same altitude, so as to give the text a stereoscopic structure. The reconstruction of the text's architecture, therefore, takes the form of a circular process, in the sense that the presupposition of a certain kind of whole is implied in the recognition of the parts. And reciprocally, it is in construing the details that we construe the whole. There is no necessity, no evidence, concerning what is important and what is unimportant. The judgment of importance is itself a guess.

Second, to construe a text is to construe it as an individual. As we saw in the second essay, if a work is produced according to generic (and genetic) rules, it is also produced as a singular being. Only *technè* generates individuals, says Aristotle, whereas *epistémè* grasps species. Kant, from another point of view, confirms this statement: the judgment of taste is only about individuals. Concretely, the work of discourse, as this unique work, can only be reached by a process of narrowing down the scope of generic concepts, which include the literary genre, the class of texts to which this text belongs, and the types of codes and structures that intersect in this text. This localization and individualization of the unique text is also a guess.

The text as a whole and as a singular whole may be compared to an object, which may be viewed from several sides, but never from all sides at once. Therefore the reconstruction of the whole has a perspectival aspect similar to that of a perceived object. It is always possible to relate the same

77

sentence in different ways to this or that other sentence considered as the cornerstone of the text. A specific kind of onesidedness is implied in the act of reading. This onesidedness grounds the guess character of interpretation.

Third, the literary texts involve potential horizons of meaning, which may be actualized in different ways. This trait is more directly related to the role of the secondary metaphoric and symbolic meanings described in the third essay than to the theory of writing developed in the second one. A few years ago I used to link the task of hermeneutics primarily to the deciphering of the several layers of meaning in metaphoric and symbolic language. I think today, however, that metaphoric and symbolic language is not paradigmatic for a general theory of hermeneutics. This theory must cover the whole problem of discourse, including writing and literary composition. But, even here, the theory of metaphor and of symbolic expressions may be said to provide a decisive extension to the field of meaningful expressions, by adding the problematic of multiple meaning to that of meaning in general. Literature is affected by this extension to the degree that it can be defined in semantic terms by the relation between primary and secondary meanings in it. The secondary meanings, as in the case of the horizon, which surrounds perceived objects, open the work to several readings. It may even be said that these readings are ruled by the prescriptions of meaning belonging to the margins of potential meaning surrounding the semantic nucleus of the work. But these prescriptions too have to be guessed before they can rule the work of interpretation.

As concerns the procedures for validation by which we test our guesses, I agree with E. D. Hirsch that they are closer to a logic of probability than to a logic of empirical verification. To show that an interpretation is more probable in the light of what we know is something other than showing that a conclusion is true. So in the relevant sense, validation is not verification. It is an argumentative discipline comparable to the juridical procedures used in legal interpretation, a logic of uncertainty and of qualitative probability. It follows from this understanding of validation that we may give an acceptable sense to the opposition between the *Naturwissenschaften* and the *Geisteswissenschaften* without conceding anything to the alleged Romanticist dogma of the ineffability of the individual. The method of converging indices, which characterizes the logic of subjective probability, provides a firm basis for a science of the individual, which may rightly be called a science. And since a text is a quasi-individual, the validation of an interpretation applied to it may be said to give a scientific knowledge of the text.

Such is the balance between the genius of guessing and the scientific character of validation, which constitutes a modern presentation of the dialectic between *verstehen* and *erlären*.

At the same time, we are also enabled to give an acceptable meaning to the famous concept of the hermeneutical circle. Guess and validation are in a sense circularly related as subjective and objective approaches to the text. But this circle is not a vicious one. That would be the case if we were unable to escape the kind of "self-confirmability" which, according to Hirsch,[3] threatens the relation between guess and validation. But to the procedures of validation there also belong procedures of invalidation similar to the criteria of falsifiability proposed by Karl Popper in his *Logic of Discovery*.[4] Here the role of falsification is played by the conflict between competing interpretations. An interpretation must not only be probable, but more probable than another interpretation. There are criteria of relative superiority for resolving this conflict, which can easily be derived from the logic of subjective probability.

To conclude this section, if it is true that there is always more than one way of construing a text, it is not true that all interpretations are equal. The text presents a limited field of possible constructions. The logic of validation allows us to move between the two limits of dogmatism and scepticism. It is always possible to argue for or against an interpretation, to confront interpretations, to arbitrate between them and to seek agreement, even if this agreement remains beyond our immediate reach.[5]

From Explanation to Comprehension

The preceding description of the dialectic between understanding as guessing and explanation as validation was roughly the counterpart of the dialectic between event and meaning. The following presentation of the same dialectic, but in the reverse order, may be related to another polarity in the structure of discourse, that of sense and reference. As I said in the first essay, this new dialectic can be considered from one point of view as an extension of the first one. The reference expresses the full exteriorization of discourse to the extent that the meaning is not only the ideal object intended by the utterer, but the actual reality aimed at by the utterance. But, from another point of view, the polarity of sense and reference is so specific that it deserves a distinct treatment, which reveals its fate in writing and, above all, in some literary uses of discourse. The same points will hold for the counterparts of the theory of the text in the theory of reading.

We have seen that the referential function of written texts is deeply affected by the lack of a situation common to both writer and reader. It exceeds the mere ostensive designation of the horizon of reality surrounding the dialogical situation. Of course, written sentences keep using ostensive devices, but these ostensive terms can no longer hold for ways of showing what is referred to. This alteration of the ostensive designation has positive and negative implications. On the one hand, it implies an extension of the referred to reality. Language has a world now and not just a situation. But, to the extent that this world, for most of its parts, has not been shown, but merely designated, a complete abstraction of the surrounding reality becomes possible. This is what happens with some works of discourse, in fact with most literary works, in which the referential intention is suspended, or at least those in which the reference to the familiar objects of ordinary discourse is suspended, to say nothing for the time being of another kind of reference to some of the more deeply rooted aspects or dimensions of our being in the world.

The new dialectic between explanation and comprehension is the counterpart of these adventures of the referential function of the text in the theory of reading. The abstraction from the surrounding world made possible by writing and actualized by literature gives rise to two opposed attitudes. As readers, we may either remain in a kind of state of suspense as regards any kind of referred to reality, or we may imaginatively actualize the potential non-ostensive references of the text in a new situation, that of the reader. In the first case, we treat the text as a worldless entity. In the second, we create a new ostensive reference thanks to the kind of "execution" that the act of reading implies. These two possibilities are equally entailed by the act of reading conceived of as their dialectical interplay.

The first way of reading is exemplified today by the various structural schools of literary criticism. Their approach is not only possible, but legitimate. It proceeds from the acknowledgement of what I have called the suspension or suppression of the ostensive reference. The text intercepts the "worldly" dimension of the discourse — the relation to a world which could be shown — in the same way as it disrupts the connection of the discourse to the subjective intention of the author. To read, in this way, means to prolong the suspension of the ostensive reference and to transfer oneself into the "place" where the text stands, within the "enclosure" of this worldless place. According to this choice, the text no longer has an exterior, it only has an interior. To repeat, the very constitution of the text as a text and of the system of texts as literature justifies this conversion of the literary object into a closed system of signs, analogous to the kind of closed system that phonology discovered underlying all discourse, and which Saussure called *langue*. Literature, according to this working hypothesis, becomes an analogon of *langue*.

On the basis of this abstraction, a new kind of explanatory attitude may be extended towards the literary object. This new attitude is not borrowed from an area of knowledge alien to language, but it comes from the same field, the semiological field. It is henceforth possible to treat texts according to the explanatory rules that linguistics successfully applied to the elementary systems of signs which underlie the use of language. We have learned from the Geneva school, the Prague

81

school, and the Danish school of linguistics that it is always possible to abstract systems from processes and to relate these systems, whether they be phonological, lexical, or syntactical, to units which are already defined through opposition to other units of the same system. This interplay of distinctive entities within finite sets of such units, as we have seen in the first essay, defines the notion of structure in modern linguistics.

It is this structural model that is now applied to texts, i.e., to sequences of signs longer than the sentence, which is the last kind of unit that linguistics takes into account.

This extension of the structural model to texts is a daring endeavor. Is not a text more on the side of *parole*—of speech—than on the side of *langue*? Is it not a succession of utterances, and therefore, in the final analysis, a succession of sentences? Did we not show in our first essay the opposition between spoken and written language, as contained in the concept of discourse which we opposed to *langue*? Such questions indicate at least that the extension of the structural model to texts does not exhaust the field of possible attitudes in regard to text. We must therefore limit this extension of the linguistic model to being just one of the possible approaches to the notion of interpreting texts. Let us, however, first consider an example of such an approach in some detail before moving on to consider a second possible conception of interpretation.

In his essay "The Structural Study of Myth," Claude Lévi-Strauss formulates the working hypothesis of structural analysis in regard to one category of texts, that of myths.[6] He says, "Myth, like the rest of language, is made up of constituent units. These constituent units presuppose the constituent units present in language when analyzed on other levels—namely phonemes, morphemes, and sememes—but they, nevertheless, differ from the latter in the same way as the latter differ among themselves; they belong to a higher and more complex order. For this reason, we shall call them *gross constituent units*."[7]

Using this hypothesis, the large units, which are at least the same size as the sentence and which, when put together, form the narrative proper to the myth, will be able to be treated according to the same rules that apply to the smallest units know to linguistics. It is to insist on this likeness that Lévi-Strauss calls them mythemes, just as we speak of phonemes, morphemes, and sememes. But in order to remain within the limits of the analogy between mythemes and the lower level units, the analysis of texts will have to perform the same sort of abstraction as that practiced by the phonologist. For the latter, the phoneme is not a concrete sound, in an absolute sense, with its acoustic quality. It is not a substance, to speak like Saussure, but a form, that is to say, an interplay of relations. Similarly, a mytheme is not one of the sentences of a myth, but an oppositive value attached to several individual sentences, which form "a bundle of relations." It "is only as bundles that these relations can be put to use and combined so as to produce a meaning."[8] What is here called a meaning is not at all what the myth means, in the sense of its philosophical or existential content or intuition, but rather the arrangement or disposition of the mythemes themselves; in short, the structure of the myth.

I would like to briefly recall here the analysis that Lévi-Strauss offers of the Oedipus myth following this method. He first separates the sentences of the myth into four columns. In the first column he places all those sentences which speak of an over-esteemed kinship relation: for example, Oedipus weds Jocasta, his mother; Antigone buries Polyneices, her brother, in spite of the order not to do so. In the second column are the same relations, but inverted as an under-esteemed kinship relation: Oedipus kills his father, Laios; Eteocles kills his brother, Polyneices. The third column is concerned with monsters and their destruction. The fourth groups together all the proper names whose meanings suggest a difficulty in walking upright: lame, clumsy, swollen foot.

Comparison of the four columns reveals a correlation. Between numbers one and two, we have kinship relationships in turn over-esteemed and under-esteemed. Between three and four, there is an affirmation and then a negation of man's autochthony. "It follows that column four is to column three as column one is to column two. . . . By a correlation of this type, the overrating of blood relations is to the underrating of blood

83

relations as the attempt to escape autochthony is to the impossibility to succeed in it."[9]

The myth thus appears as a sort of logical instrument which draws together contradictions in order to overcome them. "The inability to connect two kinds of relationships is overcome (or rather replaced) by the assertion that contradictory relationships are identical inasmuch as they are both self-contradictory in a similar way."[10]

We can indeed say that we have explained the myth, but not that we have interpreted it. We have, by means of structural analysis, brought out the logic of the operations that relate the four bundles of relationships among themselves. This logic constitutes "the structural law of the myth" under consideration.[11] It will not go unnoticed that this law is preeminently an object of reading and not at all of speaking, in the sense of a reciting where the power of myth would be re-enacted in a particular situation. Here the text is only a text, and reading inhabits it only as a text, thanks to the suspension of its meaning for us and the postponement of all actualization through contemporary discourse.

I have just cited an example from the field of myths. I could cite another from a neighboring field, that of folklore narratives. This field has been explored by the Russian formalists of the school of Propp and by the French specialists of the structural analysis of narratives, Roland Barthes and A. J. Greimas. The postulates used by Lévi-Strauss are also used by these authors. The units above the sentence have the same composition as those below it. The meaning of an element is its ability to enter into relation with other elements and with the whole work. These postulates define the closure of the narrative. The task of structural analysis therefore consists in performing a segmentation (the horizontal aspect) and then establishing various levels of integration of parts in the whole (the hierarchical aspect). But the units of action, which are segmented and organized in this way, have nothing to do with psychological traits susceptible of being lived or with behavioral segments susceptible of falling under a behaviorist psychology. The extremities of these sequences are only switching points in the narrative, such that if one element is changed, all the rest is different, too. We here recognize a transposition of the commutative method from the phonological level to the level of the narrative units. The logic of action then consists in linking together action kernels, which together constitute the narrative's structural continuity. The application of this technique results in a "dechronologizing" of the narrative, so as to make apparent the narrative logic underlying the narrative time. Ultimately, the narrative is reduced to a combination of a few dramatic units such as promising, betraying, hindering, aiding, etc., which would thus be the paradigms of action. A sequence is a succession of action kernels, each one closing off an alternative opened up by the preceding one. The elementary units, in their turn, fit in with larger units. For example, the encounter embraces such elementary actions as approaching, summoning, greeting, etc. To explain a narrative is to get hold of this symphonic structure of segmental actions.

To the chain of actions correspond similar relations between the "actors" in the narrative. By this one does not mean psychological subjects, but formalized roles correlative to the formalized actions. The actors are defined only by the predicates of action, by the semantic axes of the sentence and the narrative: the one who does the acts, to whom the acts are done, with whom the acts are done, etc. It is the one who promises, who receives the promise, the giver, the receiver, etc. Structural analysis thus brings out a hierarchy of actors correlative to the hierarchy of actions.

The next step is to assemble together the parts of the narrative to form a whole and put it back into narrative communication. It is then a discourse addressed by the narrator to a receiver. But, for structural analysis, the two interlocutors must be looked for nowhere else than in the text. The narrator is designated by the narrative signs, which themselves belong to the very constitution of the narrative. There is nothing beyond the three levels of actions, actors, and narration that falls within the semiological approach. Beyond the last level there is left only the world of the users of the narrative, which itself falls under other semiological disciplines that deal with social, economic, or ideological systems.

This transposition of a linguistic model to the theory of narrative perfectly corroborates my initial remark regarding the contemporary understanding of explanation. Today the concept of explanation is no longer borrowed from the natural sciences and transferred into a different field, that of written documents. It proceeds from the common sphere of language thanks to the analogical transference from the small units of language (phonemes and lexemes) to the large units beyond the sentence, including narrative, folklore, and myth.

This is what the structural schools mean by explanation in the rigorous sense of the term.

I now want to show in what way explanation (*erklären*) requires understanding (*verstehen*) and how understanding brings forth in a new way the inner dialectic, which constitutes interpretation as a whole.

As a matter of fact, nobody stops with a conception of myths and narratives as formal as this algebra of constitutive units. This can be shown in a number of ways. First, even in the most formalized presentation of myths by Lévi-Strauss, the units, which he calls mythemes, are still expressed as sentences, which bear meaning and reference. Can anyone say that their meaning as such is neutralized when they enter into the bundle of relations, which alone is taken into account by the logic of the myth? Even this bundle of relations must be written in the form of a sentence. In the case of the Oedipus myth, the alternation between over-evaluated and under-evaluated kinship relationships means something that has deep existential bearings. Finally, the kind of language game that the whole system of oppositions and combinations embodies would lack any kind of significance if the oppositions themselves, which Lévi-Strauss tends to mediate in his presentation of the myth, were not meaningful oppositions concerning birth and death, blindness and lucidity, sexuality and truth. Without these existential conflicts there would be no contradictions to overcome, no logical function of the myth as an attempt to solve these contradictions.[12]

Structural analysis does not exclude, but presupposes, the opposite hypothesis concerning myth, i.e., that it has meaning as a narrative of origins. Structural analysis merely represses this function. But it cannot suppress it. The myth would not even function as a logical operator if the propositions that it combines did not point towards boundary situations. Structural analysis, far from getting rid of this radical questioning, restores it at a higher level of radicality.

If this is true, could we not then say that the function of structural analysis is to lead us from a surface semantics, that of the narrated myth, to a depth semantics, that of the boundary situations, which constitute the ultimate "referent" of the myth?

I believe that if this were not the case, structural analysis would be reduced to a sterile game, a divisive algebra, and even the myth itself would be bereaved of the function Lévi-Strauss himself assigns it, that of making men aware of certain oppositions and of tending towards their progressive mediation. To eliminate this reference to the aporias of existence around which mythic thought gravitates would be to reduce the theory of myth to the necrology of the meaningless discourses of mankind.

If, on the contrary, we consider structural analysis as one stage — albeit a necessary one — between a naive interpretation and a critical one, between a surface interpretation and a depth interpretation, then it would be possible to locate explanation and understanding at two different stages of a unique hermeneutical arc.

Taking the notion of depth semantics as our guideline, we can now return to our initial problem of the reference of the text. We can now give a name to this non-ostensive reference. It is the kind of world opened up by the depth semantics of the text, a discovery, which has immense consequences regarding what is usually called the sense of the text.

The sense of a text is not behind the text, but in front of it. It is not something hidden, but something disclosed. What has to be understood is not the initial situation of discourse, but what points towards a possible world, thanks to the non-ostensive reference of the text. Understanding has less than ever to do with the author and his situation. It seeks to grasp the world-propositions opened up by the reference of the text. To understand a text is to follow its movement from sense to reference: from what it says, to what it talks about. In this process the mediating role played by structural analysis constitutes both the justification of the objective approach and the rectification of the subjective approach to the text. We are definitely enjoined from identifying understanding with some kind of intuitive grasping of the intention underlying the text. What we have said about the depth semantics that structural analysis yields rather invites us to think of the sense of the text as an injunction coming from the text, as a new way of looking at things, as an injunction to think in a certain manner.

This is the reference borne by the depth semantics. The text speaks of a possible world and of a possible way of orientating oneself within it. The dimensions of this world are properly opened up by and disclosed by the text. Discourse is the equivalent for written language of ostensive reference for spoken language. It goes beyond the mere function of pointing out and showing what already exists and, in this sense, transcends the function of the ostensive reference linked to spoken language. Here showing is at the same time creating a new mode of being.

CONCLUSION

To conclude the last essay and the whole series of essays, I want now to return to the problem raised at the end of the second essay about the dialectic of distanciation and appropriation. This dialectic has an existential overtone. Distanciation meant above all estrangement, and appropriation was intended as the "remedy" which could "rescue" cultural heritages of the past from the alienation of distance. This exchange between distance and proximity defined the historicity of interpretation in the absence of any Hegelian absolute knowledge. But at the same time I made a plea for a concept of productive distanciation, according to which the predicament of cultural distance would be transformed into an epistemological instrument. But how can distance be made productive?

The dialectic of explanation and understanding may provide an answer to the extent that it constitutes the epistemological dimension of the existential dialectic. On the basis of this dialectic, productive distance means methodological distanciation.

This active methodological distanciation finds an appropriate expression in the general trend of literary criticism and biblical criticism insofar as it yields to the anti-historicist reaction influenced by Frege and Husserl — at least the Husserl of the *Logical Investigations*. What has been labeled "historicism" is the epistemological presupposition that the content of literary works and in general of cultural documents receives its intelligibility from its connection to the social conditions of the community that produced it or to which it

was destined. To explain a text then means primarily to consider it as the expression of certain socio-cultural needs and as
a response to certain perplexities well localized in space and
time.

The "logicist" rejoinder to such "historicism" proceeded
from a rational refutation of the epistemological presupposition of historicism. For Frege and Husserl a "meaning" (and
they had in mind not the meaning of a text, but that of a
sentence) is not an idea that somebody has in his mind. It is
not a psychic content, but an ideal object which can be identified and reidentified by different individuals at different
times as being one and the same. By ideality they meant that
the meaning of a proposition is neither a physical nor a
psychic reality. In Frege's terms, *Sinn* is not *Vorstellung*, if we
call *Vorstellung* (idea, representation) the mental event linked
to the actualization of the sense by a given speaker in a given
situation. The sameness of the sense in the infinite series of its
mental actualizations constitutes the ideal dimension of the
proposition.

In a similar manner, Husserl described the content of all
intentional acts as noematic objects, irreducible to the psychic
side of the acts themselves. The notion of an ideal *Sinn* borrowed from Frege was extended in that way by Husserl to all
psychic achievements, not only to logical acts, but also to
perceptual, volitional, and emotional acts. For an objective
phenomenology, every intentional act without exception
must be described from its noematic sides as the correlate of a
corresponding noetic act.

This reversal in the theory of propositional acts has important implications for hermeneutics, inasmuch as this discipline is understood as the theory of the fixation of life-
expressions by writing. After 1900, Dilthey himself made the
utmost effort to introduce into his theory of meaning the kind
of ideality that he found in Husserl's *Logical Investigations*. In
Dilthey's late works, the inner connection (*Zusammenhang*),
which gives a text or a work of art or a document its capacity to
be understood by another person and to be fixed by writing, is
something similar to the ideality that Frege and Husserl recognized as the meaning of a proposition. If this comparison

holds, then the act of *verstehen* is less *geschichtlich* and more *logisch* than the famous article of 1900, *"Die Entstehung der Hermeneutik"* had claimed it was.[13] The whole theory of the *Geisteswissenschaften* was affected by this important shift.

Corresponding to this reversal from historicity to logicity in the general explanation of cultural expressions we may point to a similar move in the field of literary criticism, both in America and on the Continent. A wave of "anti-historicism" followed the previous excesses of psychological and sociological explanations. For this new explanatory attitude, a text is not primarily a message addressed to a specific range of readers and, in that sense, not a segment in a historical chain; inasmuch as it is a text, it is a kind of atemporal object, which has, so to speak, cut its ties from all historical development. The access to writing implies this overcoming of the historical process, the transfer of discourse to a sphere of ideality that allows an indefinite widening of the sphere of communication.

I must admit that I take this anti-historicist trend into account in my own efforts and that I agree with its main presupposition concerning the objectivity of meaning in general.

First, it is in agreement with the main concepts of this study: the semantic autonomy of written discourse and the self-contained existence of the literary work are ultimately grounded in the objectivity of meaning of oral discourse itself. Second, this anti-historicism is the implicit presupposition of the "explanatory" procedures applied by literary criticism and biblical criticism more or less under the influence of structuralism. Placed against the background of the dialectic between explanation and understanding or comprehension, the existential concept of distanciation receives an epistemological development. The text — objectified and dehistoricized — becomes the necessary mediation between writer and reader.

The existential concept of appropriation is no less enriched by the dialectic between explanation and understanding. Indeed, it must lose nothing of its existential force. To "make one's own" what was previously "foreign" remains the ultimate aim of all hermeneutics. Interpretation in its last stage wants to equalize, to render contemporaneous, to assimilate in the sense of making similar. This goal is achieved insofar as interpretation actualizes the meaning of the text for the present reader.

Appropriation remains the concept for the actualization of the meaning as addressed to somebody. Potentially a text is addressed to anyone who can read. Actually it is addressed to me, *hic et nunc*. Interpretation is completed as appropriation when reading yields something like an event, an event of discourse, which is an event in the present moment. As appropriation, interpretation becomes an event.

But the concept of appropriation is in need of a critical counterpart, which the concept of comprehension alone can bring forth. Without this epistemological complement, appropriation is in danger of being misconceived. This may happen in several ways.

According to the first misconception, appropriation appears as a return to the Romanticist claim to a "congenial" coincidence with the "genius" of the author. A return to the central analysis of the present essay is sufficient to prevent our accepting this hermeneutical prejudice. What is indeed to be understood — and consequently appropriated — in a text?

Not the intention of the author, which is supposed to be hidden behind the text; not the historical situation common to the author and his original readers; not the expectations or feelings of these original readers; not even their understanding of themselves as historical and cultural phenomena. What has to be appropriated is the meaning of the text itself, conceived in a dynamic way as the direction of thought opened up by the text. In other words, what has to be appropriated is nothing other than the power of disclosing a world that constitutes the reference of the text. In this way we are as far as possible from the Romanticist ideal of coinciding with a foreign psyche. If we may be said to coincide with anything, it is not the inner life of another ego, but the disclosure of a possible way of looking at things, which is the genuine referential power of the text.

This link between disclosure and appropriation is, to my mind, the cornerstone of a hermeneutic which would claim both to overcome the shortcomings of historicism and to remain faithful to the original intention of Schleiermacher's hermeneutics.

To understand an author better than he could understand himself is to display the power of disclosure implied in his discourse beyond the limited horizon of his own existential situation. The process of distanciation, of atemporalization, to which I connected the phase of *erklärung*, is the fundamental presupposition for this enlarging of the horizon of the text.

In this sense, appropriation has nothing to do with any kind of person to person appeal. It is instead close to what Hans-Georg Gadamer calls a fusion of horizons (*Horizonverschmelzung*): the world horizon of the reader is fused with the world horizon of the writer. And the ideality of the text is the mediating link in this process of horizon fusing.

According to a second misconception, the hermeneutical task would be ruled by the understanding of the original addressee of the text. This task as Gadamer has convincingly demonstrated is completely misconceived. The letters of Paul are no less addressed to me than to the Romans, the Galatians, the Corinthians, and the Ephesians. Only the dialogue has a "thou" whose identification precedes discourse. The meaning of a text is open to anyone who can read. The omnitemporality of the meaning is what opens it to unknown readers. Hence the historicity of reading is the counterpart of this specific omnitemporality; since the text has escaped its author and his situation, it has also escaped its original addressee. Henceforth it may provide itself with new readers. This widening of the range of readers is the consequence of the initial transgression of the first event into the universality of sense. In this sense, writing is the paradigmatic mediation between two word-events: a word-event engenders a new word-event under the condition of the overcoming of the event in the universality of the sense; this universality alone may generate new speech events.

According to a third misconception, the appropriation of the meaning of a text by an actual reader would place the

93

interpretation under the empire of the finite capacities of understanding of this reader. This objection has often been raised against all brands of "existential" hermeneutics. It has been opposed to the Heideggerian concept of *Vorverständnis* and to the restatement of the "hermeneutical circle" by Bultmann. If we must "believe" in order to "understand," then there is no difference between pre-understanding and mere projection of our prejudices.

The English (and French) translation of *Aneignung* by appropriation reinforces this mistrust: Are we not putting the meaning of the text under the power of the subject who interprets it? This objection may be removed if we keep in mind that what is "made one's own" is not something mental, not the intention of another subject, presumably hidden behind the text, but the project of a world, the pro-position of a mode of being in the world that the text opens up in front of itself by means of its non-ostensive references. Far from saying that a subject already mastering his own way of being in the world projects the *a priori* of his self-understanding on the text and reads it into the text, I say that interpretation is the process by which disclosure of new modes of being — or if you prefer Wittgenstein to Heidegger, of new forms of life—gives to the subject a new capacity for knowing himself. If the reference of the text is the project of a world, then it is not the reader who primarily projects himself. The reader rather is enlarged in his capacity of self-projection by receiving a new mode of being from the text itself.

Appropriation, in this way, ceases to appear as a kind of possession, as a way of taking hold of things; instead it implies a moment of dispossession of the egoistic and narcissistic ego. This process of dispossessing is the work of the kind of universality and atemporality emphasized in explanatory procedures. And this universality in its turn is linked to the disclosing power of the text as distinct from any kind of ostensive reference. Only the interpretation that complies with the injunction of the text, that follows the "arrow" of the sense and that tries to think accordingly, initiates a new self-understanding. In this self-understanding, I would oppose the self, which proceeds from the understanding of the text, to the ego, which claims to precede it. It is the text, with its universal power of world disclosure, which gives a self to the ego.

REFERENCE NOTES

ESSAY I

¹Ferdinand de Saussure, *Cours de linguistique générale* (Paris: Payot, 1971); English trans. by Wade Baskin, *Course in General Linguistics* (New York: McGraw-Hill, 1966).

²V. Propp, *Morphology of the Folktale* (Bloomington, Indiana: Indiana University Press, 1958).

³Edmund Husserl, *Logical Investigations*, trans. J. N. Findlay (London: Routledge & Kegan Paul, 1970), 2 vols.

⁴This point has been made forcefully and convincingly by Paul Grice. See his "Meaning," *Philosophical Review*, 66 (1957): 377-88; "Utterer's Meaning, Sentence-Meaning, and World-Meaning," *Foundations of Language*, 4 (August 1968): 225-45; "Utterer's Meaning and Intentions," *Philosophical Review*, 78 (1969): 147-77.

⁵John Searle, *Speech Acts: An Essay in the Philosophy of Language* (New York: Cambridge University Press, 1969).

⁶G. Frege, "On Sense and Reference," trans. Max Black, in *Translations from the Philosophical Writings of Gottlob Frege*, Peter Geach and Max Black (eds.) (Oxford: Basil Blackwell, 1970), pp. 56-78.

⁷P. F. Strawson, "On Referring," *Mind*, 59 (1950); 320-44. See also Bertrand Russell, "On Denoting," *Mind*, 14 (1905): 479-93; reprinted in *Logic and Knowledge: Essays 1901-1950* (London: George Allen & Unwin, 1956), pp. 39-56.

⁸Frege, op. cit., p. 61; see also p. 63.

ESSAY II

¹Jacques Derrida, *La voix et le phénomène* (Paris: Presses Universitaires de France, 1967); *L'écriture et la différence* (Paris: Seuil, 1967); *De la grammatologie* (Paris: Les Editions de Minuit, 1967); "La Mythologie blanche," *Rhétorique et philosophie*, *Poétique*, 5 (1955); reprinted in *Marges de la philosophie* (Paris: Les Editions de Minuit, 1972), pp. 247-324.

²In T. A. Sebeok (ed.), *Style in Language* (Cambridge: Massachusetts Institute of Technology Press, 1960), pp. 350-377.

[3]Martin Heidegger, *Being and Time*, trans. John Macquarrie & Edward Robinson (New York: Harper & Brothers, 1962).
[4]*Phaedrus*, 274e-277a.
[5]François Dagognet, *Ecriture et iconographie* (Paris: Vrin, 1973).
[6]For a discussion of this concept of distanciation in contemporary hermeneutics, see my article, "The Hermeneutical Function of Distanciation," *Philosophy Today*, 17:2 (Summer 1973): 129-41.

ESSAY III

[1]*The Symbolism of Evil*, trans. Emerson Buchanan (New York: Harper & Row, 1967); *Freud and Philosophy: An Essay on Interpretation*, trans. Denis Savage (New Haven: Yale University Press, 1970).
[2]Monroe Beardsley, *Aesthetics* (New York: Harcourt, Brace and World, 1958), p. 134.
[3]*Poetics*, XXI, 4.
[4]See I. A. Richards, *The Philosophy of Rhetoric* (Oxford: Oxford University Press, 1936); Max Black, *Models and Metaphors* (Ithaca, New York: Cornell University Press, 1962); Monroe Beardsley, op. cit.; Idem., "Metaphor," *Encyclopedia of Philosophy*, Paul Edwards (ed.) (New York: Macmillan, 1967), vol. 5, pp. 284-89; Idem., "The Metaphorical Twist," *Philosophy and Phenomenological Research*, 22 (1962): 293-307; Colin Turbayne, *The Myth of Metaphor* (Columbia, South Carolina: University of South Carolina Press, 1970), rev. ed.; Philip Wheelwright, *The Burning Fountain* (Bloomington, Indiana: Indiana University Press, 1968), rev. ed.
[5]Jean Cohen, *Structure du langage poétique* (Paris: Flammarion, 1966).

> [6]Time hath, my lord, a wallet at his back
> Wherein he puts alms for oblivion,
> A great-sized monster of ingratitude.
> Those scraps are good deeds past, which are devoured
> As fast as they are made, forgot as soon
> As done.

"Troilus and Cressida," III, 3, 11. 145-50. Cited in Marcus B. Hester, *The Meaning of Poetic Metaphor* (The Hague: Mouton, 1967), p. 164.

[7]Rudolf Otto, *The Idea of the Holy: An Inquiry into the Non-Rational Factor in the Idea of the Divine and its Relation to the Rational*, trans. John W. Harvey (New York: Oxford University Press, 1958).

[8]Philip Wheelwright, op. cit.; *Metaphor and Reality* (Bloomington, Indiana: Indiana University Press, 1962).

[9]Mircea Eliade, *Patterns in Comparative Religion*, trans. Rosemary Sheed (Cleveland and New York; The World Publishing Company, 1958).

[10]Max Black, op. cit.

[11]Ian Ramsey, *Models and Mystery* (New York: Oxford University Press, 1964); *Models for Divine Activity* (London: S.C.M. Press, 1973); *Religious Language* (London: S.C.M. Press, 1957).

[12]See Essay I, note 6.

[13]Mary B. Hesse, *Models and Analogies in Science* (Notre Dame, Indiana: University of Notre Dame Press, 1966).

[14]Max Black, op. cit., p. 236.

[15]Ibid., p. 238.

ESSAY IV

[1]*Critique of Pure Reason*, trans. N. K. Smith (New York: St. Martin's Press, 1965), A314, B370, p. 310.

[2]E. D. Hirsch says very convincingly, "The act of understanding is at first a genial (or a mistaken) guess and there are no methods for making guesses, no rules for generating insights. The methodological activity of interpretation commences when we begin to test and criticize our guesses." *Validity in Interpretation* (New Haven: Yale University Press, 1967), p. 203.

[3]Ibid., pp. 164-207.

[4]Karp Popper, *The Logic of Scientific Discovery* (New York: Harper & Row, 1968).

[5]In this part of my essay I have largely drawn on materials borrowed from E. D. Hirsch. I am sufficiently indebted to his

point of view to say where I disagree with him. In spite of his insistence on the mute character of the text, he maintains that the aim of the interpretation is to recognize what the author meant. "All valid interpretation, of every sort, is founded on the re-cognition of what an author meant." (p. 126) In fact, however, the intention of the author is lost as a psychical event. Moreover, the intention of writing has no other expression than the verbal meaning of the text itself. Hence all information concerning the biography and the psychology of the author constitutes only a part of the total information which the logic of validation has to take into account. This information, as distinct from the text interpretation, is in no way normative as regards the task of interpretation.

[6]In *Structural Anthropology*, trans. Claire Jacobson and Brooke Grundfest Schoepf (Garden City, New York: Anchor Books, 1967) pp. 208-28.

[7]Ibid., pp. 206-7.

[8]Ibid., p. 207.

[9]Ibid., p. 212.

[10]Ibid.

[11]Ibid., p. 214.

[12]Lévi-Strauss seems to admit this, in spite of himself, when he writes, "If we keep in mind that mythical thought always progresses from the awareness of oppositions toward their resolution, the reason for these choices becomes clearer." (Ibid., p. 221.) And again, "the myth provides a kind of logical tool." (Ibid., p. 212.) In the background of the myth there is a question which is a highly meaningful one: "Is one born from one or from two?" Even formalized in this way, "Is the same born from the same or from the other?", the question expresses anxiety and agony regarding our origin.

[13]*Gesammelte Schriften*, vol. 5., pp. 317-38.

INDEX